PSALMS
Songs of Devotion

PSALMS

Songs of Devotion

Volume 1
PSALMS 1—50

by
ROBERT ALDEN

MOODY PRESS
CHICAGO

© 1974 by
THE MOODY BIBLE INSTITUTE
OF CHICAGO

Library of Congress Cataloging in Publication Data

Alden, Robert.
  Psalms: songs of devotion.

  (Everyman's Bible commentary)
  CONTENTS: v. 1. Psalms 1-50—v. 3. Psalms 101-
150.
  1. Bible. O.T. Psalms—Commentaries. I. Title.
II. Series.

BS1430.3.A4   223'.2'07   74-15348

ISBN 0-8024-2018-4 (v. 1)

10 11 12 Printing/EP/Year 93 92 91 90 89 88

INTRODUCTION

No other Bible book has as many authors as the Psalms. And no Bible book except Genesis covers such a long period of time.

At least one psalm (90) was penned by Moses, who lived in the second millennium before Christ. Other psalms (e.g., 137) were written at least as late as the end of the Babylonian exile, some 500 years before Christ.

David is the best known and most prolific of the psalmists. If the expression "a psalm of David" in the title means that he is the author, then he is one of the most prolific of all Bible writers. That expression, however, may merely indicate that the psalm was about David or was written for him by a court poet.

Being poetry, the psalms utilize a literary form common to all Semitic poetry, called parallelism. Any psalm, and almost any verse in the Psalms, illustrates it. The writer says the same things in different words. Two such adjoining synonymous lines or stichs within a verse are a couplet.

Sometimes, however, adjoining lines are antithetical, saying contrasting things, such as in Psalm 1:6. Still other poetical devices occur and receive mention in the body of this volume.

Many commentators on the Psalms spend considerable energy trying to determine the life situation out of which the poems arose. Articles upon articles have been written to classify and categorize the Psalms into various groups. Naturally, there is much disagreement. Only a minimum of that is done here. By and large, the Psalms are without known context. Only occasionally are specific individuals, places, and events mentioned. Perhaps this lack of specificity contributes to the Psalms' popularity.

To many people the book of Psalms is simply a source of devotional material. Some people seem concerned only about the Messianic references in the Psalms. But an understanding and appreciation of the Psalter is incomplete until each Psalm is studied individually.

This first volume on the Psalms is intended to aid in the understanding of the hymnbook of ancient Israel. A commentary does not replace the Bible. It is not a paraphrase. It merely *comments* on the Scripture. An open Bible should be kept handy while reading this book.

This study seeks a balance between the obvious and the hidden, between the technical and the simple, between the historical situation and the contemporary application, between that which is old and well-known and that which is novel and perhaps provocative or even controversial.

Most of the translations are by the author, although in some instances, for the sake of accuracy or familiarity, the King James Version is used.

It is not in the New Testament that the greatest devotional literature is found but in the Old, in the book of Psalms. Because the psalmists often speak in generalities, the Psalms can be variously interpreted and widely applied. Here, more than any place in the Bible, the heartthrob of the saint is heard. Here are the most exalted expressions of God's greatness; here are the bitterest groans of the sinful and the afflicted. Here is something for everyone in every mood.

The prayer of the author is that the same Holy Spirit who moved holy men of old to pen the words of the Bible, and who has superintended its transmission over the intervening millennia, might illumine the Psalms through this commentary. Since He is also the Spirit of truth, may He also guard from misunderstanding and guide and confirm in all truth.

PSALM 1

It is appropriate that an introduction such as Psalm 1 should begin this collection of songs and poems. Two ways of life are presented immediately. First there is the way of the righteous, the blessed, the lawkeeper, the avoider of sins. On the other hand, there is the wicked, the chaff-like man, who deserves no reward with the blessed. After all is said and done, are there not but two ways of life? We either fear and love God or we do not. The latter is one of the simplest definitions of sin.

The psalm is interesting in its structure as well as universal in its application. It has the typical parallelism of phrasing found throughout the poetical books of the Old Testament. The first verse is an example of this. Three things the blessed man does not do: he does not walk in the counsel of the ungodly; he does not stand in the way of sinners; he does not sit in the seat of the scornful.

More interesting, however, is the chiastic structure of the poem. *Chiastic* means that the first and last themes or ideas reflect each other and the middle ideas reflect each other. - - A B B A. In verses (1-2) there is the blessed man deciding for righteousness and against wickedness. At the end of the poem, in verses 5-6, the blessed Lord "decides" for the righteous man and against the wicked. In the middle of the psalm two pictures are drawn by the literary artist. Verse 3 is a picture of the righteous man as a green, fruitful tree in a fertile place. Verse 4 is a picture of a wicked man who is like useless chaff, fit only to be blown away by the wind.

Looking at the psalm in more detail, one sees what the blessed and wicked ways are. The man who does not follow bad advice, stand with sinners, or spend all his time criticizing is blessed. The verbs in verse 1 present a progression: walking, standing, sitting. But the three kinds of bad people are not progressively worse. Scorners are not worse than sinners.

What does walking in the counsel of the ungodly mean? It means simply following the advice of people who do not consider God. They do not mean to be anti-godly or atheistic, but they do not fear and love God. Hence when they give advice, God's claims and commands are of little moment. This verse is especially good for young people who are facing the major decisions of life: What and where shall I study? Whom shall I marry? What shall be my career? Shall I serve God?

Taking the advice of the ungodly leads to standing where sinners stand. We might put it in these terms: Ungodly advice leads to taking a sinner's stand on spiritual and moral issues.

The last term, *scorn,* is not too common in modern English but finds its meaning in our word *mockery.* People in the "scorner's seat" criticize many things but, in particular, God's people, God's Book, and God's way. They often mock God's Son and even the Father Himself.

But the Bible does not describe good merely in negative terms, and there follows here a description of what the blessed man is like. He thinks about God and His law, the Bible. This does not mean that he is a professional Bible scholar but, rather, that throughout the day and the waking hours of the night every happening of life prompts a reflection on something in the Bible.

Verses 3-4 present two pictures: verse 3 of the blessed man and verse 4 of the ungodly man. The former is like a green and productive tree because it is planted by a river (cf. Jer 17:8). The ungodly is pictured as chaff, the refuse of the wheat-threshing operation. Bible students may be permitted to see some limited types here. The water is a source of life as Christ is our life. The unwithering leaf is the unblemished and untarnished testimony of the obedient Christian. The fruit (cf. Gal 5:22f.) in season is the regular and abundant service which we ought to render to our Lord. In the second picture, the useless, inedible chaff is fit only for destruction. This corresponds to the eternal destiny of the wicked, who are utterly lost.

The *therefore* of verse 5 introduces the conclusion. Because the wicked are like chaff, they shall not stand at the judgment—they shall not be in the congregation of the righteous. When God executes His justice they shall not be able to withstand it. In verse 1 the blessed man chose not to stand or sit with sinners; now God justly forbids the sinner to stand or sit with His chosen. He knows and loves the righteous way of the righteous man, but the ungodly way of the ungodly man leads to peril and punishment.

PSALM 2

The second psalm is well-known for at least two reasons. It is the first Messianic psalm (verse 2 has in it the word *anointed*, which is *Messiah* in Hebrew and *Christ* in Greek). When Paul preached to the Jews of Antioch in Pisida, he cited the seventh verse (Ac 13:33). This is the only numbered reference to any Old Testament passage in the New Testament.) Hebrews 1:5 and 5:5 contain the same quotation. Revelation 19 has several allusions to phrases in this

9

psalm. Psalm 2:2 may be the background of Revelation 19:19 and Psalm 2:9-10 of Revelation 19:15.

Psalm 2 has far-reaching implications and dramatic scenes. It is also interesting in its structure. The twelve verses may easily be divided into four stanzas of three verses each. In the first three verses the vicious but vain actions of the enemies of God are presented in the form of a rhetorical question. In verses 4-6 attention is focused on the almighty Sovereign of heaven and earth and His fearful reaction to hostile plots. Verses 7-9 are largely a quotation within a quotation. The Son relates His Father's instructions to Him. Finally, the last three verses are exhortations to the rulers to be obeisant and obedient to the Son. Thus we have:

> The actions of earthly rulers (1-3)
> The actions of God the Father (4-6)
> The commands to the Son (7-9)
> The commands to earthly rulers (10-12)

Note the parallelism, A A B B, and the chiasmus, A B B A. (See commentary on Psalm 1 for an explanation of these terms.)

The opening verses, which describe the actions of ungodly men, do so both in general and specific terms and with progressively more detail. The psalmist indicts the nations and the people in the first verse and the leaders of the people in the second verse. Their deeds are described in the first verse as generally mad and futile, but are narrowed down in the second verse to a specific plot to overthrow God and His Christ. The third verse gives the details of this evil plot. The same Hebrew word lies behind the "meditate" of Psalm 1:2 as the word "rage" in Psalm 2:1. Whereas the godly man uses his mental energies delighting in God's Word, the ungodly leaders use theirs to plot against God's rule.

This description of the unfortunate and uninformed state

10

of the unregenerate mind is not unique to 1000 B.C. when David lived. The same thought patterns prevail more or less openly today. The world is at enmity with God, and rulers and ruled alike seek to escape the demands of God on their lives. They seek to outwit the Creator and to undo the mission of His dear Son.

The picture of God in the fourth verse is an unusual one. He laughs and derides. The laugh seems to be the kind of chuckle a champion gives when his opponent's defeat is imminent. The derision is probably mixed with the wrath and displeasure described in the following verse. He laughs at the futility of human actions, but He is angry at the whole idea of man trying to overthrow God. Rather than surrender His dignity, He commissions His king to execute wrath.

Because of the sixth verse, many liberal commentators see David and David only in this psalm. They call it a royal psalm and say it was probably composed for the enthronement of the monarch. The kingship of Israel was a divinely appointed office. The king was "set" or installed because of God's choice and was there to rule on God's behalf.

Such a limited application, however, is incompatible with the remainder of the psalm. Unless the accomplishments and promises of the Son are great exaggerations, they cannot apply to David, but only to David's greater Son, the Lord Jesus Christ. For this reason, and because the inspired authors of the New Testament so understood it, this psalm speaks of the commission and mission of Jesus the Messiah.

It helps to understand the third section of the psalm by supplying quotation marks in verses 7-9. The whole section is spoken by the Son, but He quotes His Father beginning with the words, "Thou art my Son." There is some question as to whether verse 7 should read "the decree of the LORD" or, "the decree: the LORD said."

The words of the decree itself are all-important. God says

11

to the Messiah, "Thou art my Son; this day have I begotten thee." Besides being an argument for at least two persons of the Trinity being mentioned in the Old Testament, it is also a statement of the relationship between these two persons. Paul used this verse in Acts 13:33 to support the resurrection of Christ. The Father offers the Son, for the asking, the world for an inheritance. The rebellious nations of verse 1 become the property of the Son. This truth is missionary as well as Messianic. Any passage which speaks of the ends of the earth in the plans of God is missionary. Here, however, more of the negative, judicial aspect of the Son's task is in view. Since the nations are rebels, He will smash them as one would smash a clay pot with an iron rod. The only way to avoid this wrathful punishment is to obey the commands of the last quarter of the psalm.

Verses 10-12 contain five commands to leaders of the nations: be wise, be instructed, serve the Lord, rejoice, and kiss the Son. A colloquial translation might render the first two: "Wise up; get smart." With such enlightened attitudes and divinely illumined spirits they then could serve, rejoice, and kiss the Son.

Perhaps the typical Protestant church needs verse 11b underscored: "Rejoice with trembling." We sometimes forget that it is possible to put these two things side by side. Often when we rejoice we lose our sense of dignity, and when we fear God we forget to enjoy our positions of sonship.

The translators of the Revised Standard Version presumed additional letters in the Hebrew text in order to produce their translation at this point: "Kiss his feet." The presence of the Aramaic word for son (*bar* rather than the Hebrew *ben*) perplexed them, but in recent years discoveries have shown that Aramaic is an older language than was thought. It is older than the writing of this psalm, and therefore it is not impossible that such a loan word could appear at this point, as the ancient inspired author sought for variety and color. Hence the older original reading, "Kiss the Son," is preferred. It means to do obeisance to Him. This is not the romantic kiss but the kiss on the feet, the hand, or the shoulder. His worshipers should reverence Him as vassals honored an ancient earthly sovereign. The word *little* may be a limitation of time or of quantity; that is, God's wrath may "soon" be kindled (NASB), or it may be kindled "but a little" (KJV). There are good reasons for either translation. The major concern ought to be that God be neither a little displeased with us nor soon be angered by us.

The last phrase describes the believer's place of blessedness. One arrives there by putting his trust in God. And so Psalm 2 ends with a promise, using the same line of thought with which Psalm 1 begins: "Blessed are all they that put their trust in him."

PSALM 3

The third psalm is the first one with a title. Mystery surrounds the origin of psalm titles. In most instances the title pertains to the contents of the psalm. Psalm 51 is a good example. The contents of Psalm 3 could describe any of several tight circumstances which David experienced.

The word rendered "psalm" in this title appears fifty-seven times in other titles. In most of these instances the Hebrew word describing the kind of a psalm is merely transliterated: *Shiggaion* (Ps 7), *Michtam* (Ps 16), and *Maschil* (Ps 78). There is no reason not to believe that Psalm 3 describes David's sentiments toward his son Absalom (2 Sam 15-18), as the inscription indicates.

Selah first occurs in this psalm, where it is found three

13

times. Although many suggestions have been made as to the meaning of this little word, it remains quite uncertain. It is probably a musical notation having something to do with the tempo, volume, or accompaniment of the song, or with the participation or posture of the singer. All attempts to translate it have been unfortunate and ill-advised. For the sake of symmetry one would expect a *selah* after verse 6, but there is none.

Psalm 3 falls into the category of "trouble and trust" psalms, and is one of the shorter ones. David begins by crying out to God about his troubles, which come primarily in the form of enemies (vv. 1-2). Then follows a personal testimony of God's past favors and grace. Finally, as if to say, "Do it again, Lord," the psalmist prays for salvation for himself and blessing on his people.

The emphasis in the complaint section is on the great number of enemies (cf. 2 Sam 17:1). Three times the Hebrew root for *many* occurs (translated "increased" in verse 1). Not only are these multitudes the enemies of David, but they are enemies of his God as well. Their accusation betrays this as they falsely charge, "There is no help for him in God." The word for *help* is the same word as *salvation* elsewhere (v. 8). Certainly these enemies had in mind temporal, physical salvation, although David might have meant his spiritual salvation as well. A similar range of meaning inheres in the word translated *soul*. Sometimes it means simply "breath." At other times the life principle is meant.

The testimony section begins, in general terms, in verse 3. God, says David, is my shield (cf. Gen 15:1), my glory, and the lifter up of my head. The verb *lift* may echo an earlier use of the term in verse 1. Although his enemies rose up, God raised him yet higher. Verses 4-5 mention particular features of his deliverance. In the past he cried and God heard. In the past he slept soundly and God preserved him.

14

Hence, with this new challenge, he testifies that he will not be afraid of myriads of hostile people all around him.

Some early Church Fathers saw the death and resurrection of Christ in verse 5, but most commentators see in these words simply a morning prayer.

The third section (vv. 7-8) contains a prayer for deliverance, but also includes statements of God's past accomplishments. Two verbs form the basis of the prayer: *arise* and *save*. Then, as if to remind God of His ability, the psalmist states how God had smashed the jaws and broken the teeth of former enemies. He thus likens his adversaries to disarmed animals, their weapons of destruction (jaws and teeth) now destroyed.

The last verse is somewhat like a benediction, but it is also a prayer. Salvation is God's. And since it is, the blessing is the people's. There is no salvation apart from God and He ever wants to give His people His blessing.

PSALM 4

Two additional technical terms are found in the title of Psalm 4. The *choirmaster* or *chief musician* occurs first and then the name of a musical instrument or a melody, *Neginoth,* follows. This, too, is a psalm by or about David, as the last two words of the title indicate.

It is difficult to know whom the author is addressing except in those verses where he clearly is petitioning God. Specifically, who are the "sons of men" in verse 2? Usually this term simply means "men" in the frailty of their human limitations (cf. Ps 8:4, Gen 6:2), including their propensity to sin. Were these merely the enemies of David, or did the inspired penman have all men in mind? Apparently the psalm is addressed to all men, for, apart from taking the advice of verses 3 and 4, all men love vanity and seek lies (which is the meaning of the word *leasing,* v. 2, in the KJV).

The psalm begins and ends with addresses to God. In the middle section (vv. 2-6) are admonitions to men.

The first verse is something of an introduction. There are three imperative verbs in this one verse: *answer* (rendered "hear" in the KJV), *have mercy,* and *hear.* In a manner typical of many prayers in the Bible, David reminds God of past deliverances. Things were tight for God's servant, but the Lord had released him and loosed the tension.

The first words directed to David's human audience are words of rebuke and reprimand. The three phrases are clipped and abrupt. To make the meaning understandable to the non-Semitic mind, translators must add phrases such as those indicated by italics in the King James Version. The "sons of men" turn the psalmist's glory into shame, they love vanity, they seek lies. Perhaps that first sin is their mocking or insulting David's God and making light of his devotion. (For a discussion of *selah,* see commentary on Psalm 3.)

In the rough chiastic arrangement of this psalm, verse 6 corresponds to verse 2. Again, David complains of those who ask ridiculing questions about his faith. Many of them wonder if there is any good any more. Assuming that their words continue through the end of the verse, they also ask whether God would lift up His countenance on them.

The central portion, verses 3-5, contains words of instruction. Count the commands: know, stand in awe, sin not, commune, be still, sacrifice, and trust. In verse 3 David wishes that we might know that God sovereignly sets apart the godly for Himself. It is interesting that coupled with that truth is the one regarding our ability to call on Him. So on the one hand God calls, or sets apart, the godly and on

16

the other hand He hears those who call on Him. In the one instance God initiates the action, and in the other man does.

The next four imperatives have to do with personal, private devotion. The first Hebrew word of verse 4 is rare and its translation here is uncertain. The Septuagint has "be angry." This is apparently the basis of Paul's use of the verse in Ephesians 4:26.

Perhaps if *selah* seems appropriate anywhere it is here, in view of the words "be still" which precede.

Verse 5 speaks of public worship: Offer sacrifices. Then 5b has the final and yet most basic instruction: Trust in the LORD (cf. Ps 37:5 and Pr 3:5-6). Sacrifices without trust are of no use. Works without faith are dead.

Having experienced God's salvation and continuing mercy and care, David concludes the psalm with two verses of praise. In terms understandable to farmers, he says that he is happier than at harvest. In contrast to this overt jubilation is his quiet confidence that lets him sleep soundly while God watches over his safety. *Peace* is a word loaded with meaning. One English word cannot do justice to *shalom*. Included in it are the ideas of economic and physical satisfaction, of health, and of peace with God and men. All this was possible in David's day and is also possible in ours because the LORD makes us dwell in safety.

PSALM 5

Like Psalm 3, Psalm 5 also may be a prayer or song for morning devotions, as verse 3 suggests. Like the other psalms in the beginning section of this book, it is a mixture of praise and prayer to God combined with complaints about enemies and about wicked men in general.

17

The title is similar to that of Psalm 4. Both have to do with the chief musician. But instead of being played on some stringed instrument (*Neginoth*) this poem is for the *Nehiloth*, which may mean "flutes."

The psalm has no easily discernible outline. Verses 1-3 and 8 are petitions. Four through six speak of God and His hatred of sin. Verse 7 contrasts the righteous behavior of the psalmist with the description of evildoers in the preceding verses and in verses 9 and 10. Verses 11 and 12 are a kind of benediction, which both admonishes and intercedes for the believer and praises God.

Three parallel but unbalanced lines, plus one odd line, make up the first two verses. *Give ear, consider,* and *hear* are the primary verbs. *My words, my meditation,* and *my cry* are the objects. O LORD, *my King,* and *my God* are the three vocatives. The words "consider my meditation" (or literally "groaning") in verse 1 are richer if understood as prayer that God will interpret those unintelligible noises that come from deep thought. The psalmist prays that God will understand (Ro 8:26f.).

Verse 3 indicates that the psalm may have been composed for morning worship (cf. Ps 3:5). If not, it may simply show that the psalmist considered prayer important enough to put early in his daily schedule.

Unlike the preceding psalms, where some verses are directed to the readers, this psalm in its entirety is addressed to God. The psalmist's complaints are not to men but to God. He urges not men but God. He communes not with men but with God. Even the criticism of the wicked is put in the form of praise: "The foolish shall not stand in thy sight; Thou hatest the workers of iniquity" (v. 5).

In verse 6*a* is the only instance, in this psalm, of the psalmist's speaking of God in the third person. There he mentions what God Himself already knows. It is another instance of the one praying reminding God of His faithfulness. Later, in verse 10, he demands that God, who abhors unrighteousness, cast out the transgressors.

David asserts his own good intentions in verse 7. This is in contrast to the debauchery and deceit of the wicked described in the two preceding verses (5-6). In both Hebrew and English, verse 7 is a *chiasmus,* although translators have somewhat revised the structure. Literally it would read:

But I,
>   in the multitude of thy mercies,
>   I will come to thy house
>   I will worship at thy holy temple
>   in thy fear.

Following this interjection of praise, David prays specifically for direction (v. 8). After that, he again launches into a diatribe against the wicked. Apparently David had been the object of much verbal abuse. Verse 9 contains his counter invective. Paul used elements of this verse in Romans 3:13 where he, too, describes the wickedness of men.

Then in verse 10, with strong passion, David as much as commands God to destroy his enemies, to let them fall, and to cast them out. Then from a different viewpoint, he focuses on the righteous and prays that they might have cause to rejoice, to shout, and to be joyful (v. 11).

Verse 12 concludes the psalm on a note of assurance, with complete faith that the Judge of all the earth will do right (cf. Gen 18:25). From past experience, and simply because he believes in the God to whom he prays, the psalmist boldly says, "With favor wilt thou compass [the righteous] as with a shield" (cf. Ps 3:3).

PSALM 6

In the title of Psalm 6 is another uncertain musical term. *Sheminith* is related to the word for *eight* and so may refer to the eight strings of a musical instrument, or to an eight-noted melody to which the psalm was sung. Perhaps it is an ancient reference to the octave.

Psalm 6 is a kind of personal lament. The classification "trouble and trust" aptly describes this psalm, as well as many others. Toward the end, however, there is a note of hope.

The psalmist begins with a recitation of his troubles. That prompts prayer for deliverance, which culminates in an affirmation of faith and confidence of victory. The more we focus on God and His greatness the more insignificant our troubles become. Many believers let their problems block their view of God. Psalms such as this should remind us that He is the God of the impossible and He summons us to cast our burdens on Him and to spread our concerns before Him.

The source of trouble in this psalm seems to be both from within and without. The first three verses sound like a confession of sin, while mention of adversaries appears in verse 7 and following. We are always our own worst enemy. Even Paul often did that which he did not want to do (Ro 7:15). We certainly need God's help to overcome the old nature.

It may be that the psalmist is equating his enemies' onslaughts with God's punishment of his sins. This raises the larger question as to whether God immediately punishes the believer for his sins. The believer must discern between punishment for wrongdoing through the chastening hand of a loving heavenly Father and the malicious attacks of Satan, the accuser of the brethren. This was Job's dilemma.

The actual content of the psalm raises some interesting

questions. From the first three verses, one might wonder to what extent grief affects physical well-being. In verse 2 the psalmist is withered and troubled in his "bones." The word "vexed," or "troubled," appears again in verse 3 and describes his soul. "Soul" recurs in verse 4 as the focus of God's deliverance. *Bones* frequently indicates one's inmost being.

Verse 5 raises the question of the psalmist's view of the afterlife. The Hebrew word *Sheol* here is parallel to "death." Often it is rendered "grave" and occasionally "hell." The psalmist is not denying consciousness after death. Rather he is saying that those who praise and thank God are the living. He is not addressing himself to the question of a conscious afterlife; rather, he is pleading with God for length of this life.

Perhaps the *withering* (KJV, weak) of verse 2 is to be understood with the profuse and bitter weeping of verses 6 and 7. So much water has flowed from the eyes of the grieved that he is literally drying up. As an adjective, this form of the word occurs only once in the Bible.

The turning point of this psalm is in the middle of verse 8, the first half of which is an imperative. The second half is declarative. It is almost as if a certain assurance of answered prayer suddenly flooded the psalmist. Why should he groan and complain any longer? The LORD has heard the sound of his weeping; He has heard his supplication; He will receive his prayer. These statements are the essence of the "trust" mentioned in this psalm. How the Lord, who has heard, will act is recited in the last verse. His enemies shall be shamed and troubled. The very words in verse 3a which describe his soul's condition now describe his foes in verse 10a. Now they shall be "greatly troubled."

In the course of this psalm the writer moves closer to God and thus relatively further from his enemies. God and the psalmist's adversaries are rather fixed entities in this drama. It is the psalmist whose position changes. When he is far from God, he is in jeopardy. But as he moves toward God, his enemy is disadvantaged, and the psalmist has his twofold problem solved. His fellowship with God is restored—the problem of the opening verses—and his vulnerability to his enemies is lessened. This pattern is the same for the Christian in his relationship to his Lord and to the enemies of the cross.

PSALM 7

Psalm 7 is called a *Shiggaion* of David. That technical Hebrew term occurs only twice in the Bible. Habakkuk 3:1 has the plural form, a verb meaning "to wander," which has the same root but does not explain anything about this psalm. It is best to offer no guesses.

Cush the Benjamite is not mentioned elsewhere in the Bible. He was probably a henchman of King Saul. This psalm probably comes out of the experiences narrated in 1 Samuel, when Saul relentlessly sought to destroy David.

Psalm 7 fits into the same category as the preceding one. It is, however, longer and more complicated. The mention of enemies appears again and again (vv. 1, 5, 6). Likewise, affirmations of trust in God occur throughout the psalm (vv. 1, 8, 9, 10, 11).

Verse 1 opens with a declaration of belief and trust. The Lord was David's God and in Him he took refuge. Then follows an imperative verb, a prayer, "Save me." Saul had shown himself ruthless before, and David feared he would be so again. He compared the king with a lion. From a poetic standpoint, notice *deliver* at the end of the first and

22

second verses. In modern, nonpoetic language we might say, "Save me while you can." These two verses are the essence of the psalm. The rest is elaboration on the two themes presented here: "The Lord is my God" and "Save me from my enemies."

Verses 3-5 are something of a self-imprecation. The writer calls curses on himself if he is not a man of integrity. The word *if*, which occurs three times, invites examination from God. The implication—rather, the assertion is that he has no evil; he has not done wrong. Having vindicated and exonerated himself and concluded with a *selah*, he continues to pray. Verses 6-9 are filled with appeals that God should act on his behalf: *Arise, lift up, awake, judge*—and so forth. Even as the psalmist pleads his own righteousness in the verses above, so here he founds his case on God's justice. Note the number of occurrences in verse 8-11 of such terms as *judgment, judge, righteousness, integrity,* and *upright*.

The subjects of the verbs in verse 12 appear ambiguous, but most agree on an indefinite subject for the first verb. God is the subject of the ensuing verbs. The import is that, if the wicked man will not repent, God will whet His sword and punish him. But in verse 14 the wicked man is again the subject. Words usually used to describe childbearing appear here to describe the production of evil. Everything goes wrong for the wicked. He falls into the pit he dug to trap others, and all his evil plans backfire.

As if David saw victory already accomplished, he closes the psalm on a note of thanksgiving and praise. Once more he mentions the justice of God—the basis on which the evil are punished and the righteous are acquitted, justified, and avenged.

PSALM 8

Psalm 8 is one of the better-known psalms. The almost identical opening and closing verses often have been put to music. The fourth verse is well-known because the author of Hebrews quotes it and applies it to Jesus Christ.

The meaning of the word *Gittith* in the title of the psalm is unknown. Neither context nor related words reveals what it means. Psalms 81 and 84 use the word and they are works of jubilant praise. The two most common suggestions are that it is a tune or a musical instrument.

The psalm falls easily into the following chiastic outline:

> A   God's excellent name (1)
>   B   God's rule (2-3)
>   C   Man's meanness (4)
>   C   Man's greatness (5)
>   B   Man's rule (6-8)
> A   God's excellent name (9)

The first half of the first verse is identical to the entire last verse and so these two elements are coupled in the outline. The two longer sections marked "B" describe God's rule and man's rule, respectively. The two middle verses (4, 5) are direct contrasts. First there is man's low view of himself as compared to God and then God's view of man.

The first verse is more extensive than the last. It states that God's name is excellent and worthy to be adored over all the earth, but it also states that His glory is set in the heavens. The latter part of verse 1 may belong with the next section of the outline.

From the suckling baby described in verse 2 on up to the highest heavens, God is Lord of all. Verse 2 is often recalled when a child says something very profound. Sometimes in their naivete children pronounce great truths which adults know but forget. One fall evening the neighbor children were playing beside our house. As it grew dark one of them said they should go home, but another responded: "Why should we be afraid of the dark? God's here." This is the meaning of Psalm 8:2. The expression *babes and sucklings* may indicate children old enough to talk. Hebrew mothers often nursed their babies for four or five years.

The purpose of using such feeble instruments to announce God's glory is to offend the adversary. How many unbelievers have been rebuked by the innocently offered remark of a child schooled in the basics of God-fearing living! When the children sang "Hosanna" on Psalm Sunday, Jesus reminded the people of this verse (Mt 21:16).

From the earthbound sphere of children, verse 3 lifts our attention to the heavens. They are the work of God's fingers. He has ordained the various heavenly bodies. The word "when" connects this verse very closely with the next.

Having focused the reader's attention on the heavens, the psalmist then wonders what dealings God would ever have with man. Why should a mortal be thought of or visited by Deity? The fifth verse answers that question immediately. It is because man is really just a little lower than God. The Hebrew word usually means "God," sometimes it means "gods," and, in a few instances, "angels." The point is that man is not just a little higher than the animals but a little lower than heaven.

Hebrews 2:6-8 quotes this passage and applies it to Christ. That New Testament passage shows that Christ is superior to angels. But because it seems to say much the opposite (the Greek word in Hebrews is "angels" and not "God"), some take the word "little" to refer to time. According to that interpretation, He was for a little while lower than the angels. This is supported by the commentary that follows in Hebrews 2:9. Psalm 8 doubtlessly is speaking of all men in general, but the writer of Hebrews, by divine inspiration, refers specifically and specially to Jesus Christ, the Son of Man and the Son of God.

Man, and particularly Jesus Christ, is crowned with glory and honor. His is a glory far grander than ours; nevertheless, the psalm can refer to both. God made everything in the world, and man is to rule it. Verse 6 says this in general terms and verses 7-8 in specific terms. Remember the chiastic arrangement of this psalm and note the references to the heavens in verses 3 and 8. God made the heavens; man is in control over the birds of the heavens.

The benediction which opened the psalm is repeated in the last verse. This time it has more meaning. God is worthy of more praise because of His love and concern for His creatures, including man. We are exalted to be His vicegerent. We, of all His creatures, are able to offer intelligent and voluntary praise. The Lord is our Lord. How excellent is His name in all the earth!

PSALM 9

Praise is the theme of Psalm 9, though the psalmist several times mentions his enemies and their certain destruction along with all the wicked. In the thirteenth and in the last two verses are brief petitions to God. But the main focus is on God Himself and His greatness.

Two technical terms appear in this psalm. First, the title indicates that it is *on* or *set to Muth-labben*. As with the other uncertain words in the titles, it is best to consider this one to signify either a tune or an instrument. There are many suggestions in ancient versions and modern commentaries which translate the words and make a connection between the contents of the psalm and some event in David's life. These suggestions are not very convincing, especially those which rely on altering the Hebrew spelling. The psalm itself speaks in general terms making it difficult to link it with a specific historical happening.

The second technical term is at the end of verse 16 where *Higgaion* appears with *selah*. As with *selah* (see commentary on Psalm 3), we were uncertain about *Higgaion*. It seems to belong to the same root as the word usually translated as "meditate." Verse 16b however, does not mark a division in the psalm, and the terms may be musical notations with relatively nothing to do with the meaning of the poem.

Another peculiarity of Psalm 9 is that it is an alphabetic acrostic when joined with Psalm 10. Apart from some minor irregularities, every second verse begins with a consecutive letter of the Hebrew alphabet.

Four *I will's* mark the first two verses. Actually, there are five things the psalmist determines to do: give thanks, show forth, be glad, exult, and sing praise. God and His work, of course, are the objects of all these verbs.

Verses 3-6 constitute the second section. Although the ancient worshiper continues to strike a note of praise, it is praise for the destruction of the enemy. This theme appears again in verses 15-17. At first, the "enemy" is the personal enemy of the psalmist. Later the terminology becomes more general. In verse 4, the jubilation over destroyed foes is interrupted, and David exults in his own vindication and justification.

Something should be said about the word *nations* (often "heathen" in KJV). It occurs in verses 5, 15, 17 and in many places in other Psalms. The Hebrew word is *goiim* and is known by anyone having close Jewish acquaintances. The oldest meaning is *"nation"* in the sense of an ethnic

27

group. Any political overtone is definitely secondary. Later the term came to mean all peoples other than Israelites, as today it means non-Jews. *Gentile* is a perfectly accurate translation but is often misunderstood. *Heathen* suggests someone from a primitive part of the world. *Nations* is the best meaning as long as it is not understood politically. Hebrew writers used *kingdom, house,* or the name of the political entity itself when they had governments in mind. *Goiim* is not so used, as the verses before us illustrate. The nations are here paralleled to the wicked, i.e., to wicked people.

The *name* at the end of verse 5 and the *remembrance* or *memorial* at the end of verse 6 point to another peculiarity of Semitic thought. A man's name is the man. His remembrance is his eternal life. That his name be blotted out and the remembrance of his acts perish is tantamount to being punished forever.

The psalmist changes focus in verse 7. The next three verses are not so much human expressions of praise as theological explanations of God and His justice. They are praise, nevertheless. The first declares God's eternality. Then follow three statements about His justice. The beneficiaries of His righteous judgment come into view in verses 8 and 9. The oppressed will find their advocate and defender in the Judge of all the earth. He will do right (Gen 18:25). Verse 9, incidentally, is a fine example of progressive parallelism. ABC BDE is the pattern. The words *high tower* (or *refuge,* KJV) connect the two stichs.

The tower of a Palestinian town was the citadel, the innermost military stronghold. While the poor and oppressed were ordinarily forbidden its protection, they can find deliverance in the Lord.

Verses 10, 11, and 12 are the center of the psalm. These three verses capsulize the entire hymn. Included are a statement of faith, a declaration of God's attributes—His justice, in particular—and an injunction to praise.

Verse 13 is a prayer. It comes right after the statement that God remembers the poor or afflicted. David identifies himself with the afflicted and so justifies his petition. Then follows his promise to praise God faithfully.

The next section contains verses 15-18 and corresponds to verses 3-6. Reports and predictions about the fate of the wicked, who bring trouble onto themselves, fill this part of the psalm. In verse 17, *nations* should be understood simply as "unbelievers."

The psalm concludes with five petitions to God. First is the positive appeal for God to arise. Then there is the negative, "Let not man prevail." Verse 19b puts the two together. Verse 20 continues the parallel with 19b. Both *nations* (or *heathen*) and *man* occur twice in these two verses. The point of the prayer is that God will fulfill His responsibility as Judge and that men should fulfill their responsibility in submissive trusting.

PSALM 10

Psalm 10 is the second half of the alphabetic acrostic that begins in Psalm 9. The natural division of this psalm falls after verse 11. Up to that point the psalmist describes the wicked. Beyond that point is the prayer to overthrow the wicked and to exonerate the righteous.

The opening verse is a complaint: "Why do You stand at a distance, Lord?" People do not want to get involved as witnesses to accidents. They walk on the other side of the road, as the priest and the Levite of the good Samaritan parable (Lk 10:30f.), when they see trouble. God, the psalmist charges, is only a fair-weather friend to the righteous. "Why do You hide Yourself in times of trouble?"

Verses 2-11 describe in detail the devious paths of the wicked man, but only in verse 2*b* is there an imprecation against him. Evil men are proud, boastful, and covetous. The word translated "blesseth" (v. 3) in the King James Version is interesting. The American Standard Version renders that Hebrew word with its polar or opposite meaning, "renounce." Several Hebrew words and several English words have such opposite meanings. "Stone" and "destone" are the same in Hebrew. "Go" and "come" may translate the same Hebrew word. Our English "let" can have opposite meanings.

Notice the arrogance of the wicked man's statements and thoughts in verses 4, 5, and 11. Not only does he say that God will not require anything of him, but he even thinks there is no God. He is more than a practical atheist—one who acts as if there is no God; he actually says there is none (v. 4b, ASV). Yet that same wicked man declares that the God who does not exist has forgotten and hidden His holy face from those wicked deeds.

The metaphor of verses 9-10 illustrates the general statements of verse 8. The wicked man says and does what is false and wrong. His victims are the poor and the weak. As a lion preys on weak, slow, or ignorant animals, so the wicked takes every unfair advantage to gain mastery over other men.

The prayer of verse 12 through the end of the psalm is a welcome relief from the grim picture in the first half. The psalmist says in so many words, "Are You going to stand for this, Lord? Do something! Have You forgotten the poor and the weak? Will You tolerate this blasphemy?"

Verse 14 provides another instance of the psalmist exerting pressure on God with the lever of historical precedent.

The helpless formerly committed their cause into God's hand and He delivered them. Will the Father of mercies now be untrue to Himself?

The strongest verse in the entire psalm is 15. Forgetting all courtesy and tolerance, the psalmist urges God to break the wicked man's arm—and so to divest him of his power. He strongly appeals to the Lord to uncover every wicked facet of this iniquitous operation. God should leave no stone unturned in order to root out evil and to right wrong.

Verses 16 to the end of the psalm are the benediction. They are written as if the prayer were already answered. The nations, unbelieving outsiders, are punished, while the meek are helped. The orphan and the oppressed will be vindicated and protected. The ravisher of the poor man's meager means will be a terror no more.

PSALM 11

Psalm 11 is another psalm of David for the chief musician. The theme is that God is a refuge from wicked men, a defense against their evil deeds. A lesson as simple as this is easily forgotten. Even Christians often fight fire with fire and sword with sword. In some very critical battles they forget that God has promised to be their refuge and defense. He delights to shield them and is honored by their requests for Him to do so.

Psalm 11 has several cryptic phrases which cannot be translated with certainty. The first is in the opening verse. Whom does the psalmist quote? Or who says the words, "Flee, bird, to your mountain"? How far should that quotation be carried? None of these questions has a certain answer, but it seems best to understand that the psalmist is

31

referring to an evil taunt. "Bird," then, was a derogatory term as it is today when used to describe a person. The *New English Bible* seems right in carrying the quote through verse 2. The wicked is warning the believer, whom he calls a bird, to get out of the way because he has readied his bow to shoot down the prey.

The first two verses, taken as a whole, are a profession of faith in the face of threat. The God-fearing writer as much as says that he is not going to be intimidated by the challenges and warnings of the wicked, since he has put his faith in God.

Verse 3 is another difficult verse. The basic meaning of all the Hebrew words is clear, but not the syntax—how they are put together. The tenses are uncertain. The nature of the subjunctive is unsure. Should it be rendered *if, when, for,* or *since?* The word *can* is only in the text by implication. And there yet remains the question, "Foundations" of what? Society? True religion? Some literal building?

Some versions, such as the Revised Standard Version, understand this as part of the wicked man's taunt and close the quotation marks at the end of verse 3. Otherwise it sounds like a confession of despair. The good man apparently admits he can do nothing in light of the bad man's destruction of that which is vital and basic. If this latter is the better interpretation, then it forms an appropriate conclusion to the first part, the negative part of the psalm.

Immediately follows the only suitable answer. Remember that God is still on the throne. Though the walls seem to crumble around us, He is still there, watching, remembering, storing up judgment. Verse 4 begins the description of God, the object of the psalmist's trust. The God of all right will always do right. There are no English synonyms for "eye," so after the word is used once, the parallel Hebrew word is translated with the strange-sounding agent of God's justice,

32

His "eyelids"! Some modern versions paraphrase to avoid this difficulty.

God tries or examines all men and all their deeds, good and bad. Especially will He put the wicked—those who love violence—on trial. God hates violence.

The picture in verse 6 is vivid and reminds us of the judgment on Sodom and Gomorrah, as well as of the fire and brimstone of Revelation 14:10, 19:20, 20:10, and 21:8.

The other side of the coin of God's perfect justice is His reward to the upright (v. 7). Since God is right and loves right deeds, He also loves righteous people. The greatest prize the poet can think of is to see God face to face.

Several gospel songs echo this hope. Carrie E. Breck (1855-1934) wrote one entitled "Face to Face." Another by Charles H. Gabriel (1856-1932) includes the lines:

> When by His grace I shall look on His face,
> That will be glory, be glory for me.

PSALM 12

Psalm 12 is a chiasmus. The first and last verses contain the phrase "sons of men" (cf. ASV) and the basic contents of these two verses are parallel. The second verse describes the words of wicked men while the sixth and seventh verses describe the pure words of the Lord. The middle verses (3, 4, 5) portray the punishment God will pour out on the wicked and the deliverance He will give to the oppressed.

Psalm 12 is in the "trouble and trust" category. Because of the chiastic structure it is "trouble-trust-trouble."

Apart from the arrangement of the themes within the psalm there are vivid word pictures drawn by the ancient artist. In fact, the cutting off of lips and the severing of tongues may have been a method of torture common to those times. The figure of the mouth is not abandoned until the end of verse 5. Whereas the wicked talks himself into trouble with God, the oppressed pant after His righteousness.

In the psalms it is common to personify a virtue, a vice, or a condition. Righteousness is the righteous man; wickedness is the wicked man; poverty is the poor man; and so on. The faithful man stands for faith. Neighbor stands for society. This psalm is a mixture of such concepts and pictures.

Verse 1 does not make it clear whether godliness or the godly man has ceased, or if righteous deeds or righteous men fail. Of course it is not crucial to the understanding of the psalm, but it is fascinating to see how concepts are actualized, and vice versa.

The psalmist's complaint is that bad men are everywhere and good men cannot be found. He has an attitude similar to Elijah's. Elijah thought he was the only believer left when, in fact, God still had 7,000 others (1 Ki 19:14, 18).

For three verses the focus is on what the wicked say. Often our enemies hurt us more by what they say than by inflicting physical harm. James warned Christians that they are not exempt from commiting sins of the tongue (3:5-10). Verse 2 contains an interesting Hebraism. Where we read with a "double heart" the original has "with heart and heart." That means that first he speaks from one set of principles and then from another.

Through the blasphemous din God still hears the groaning and gasping of the needy and oppressed. And the God of justice promises safety to these downtrodden objects of His love.

Verse 7 presents a textual problem. The verse might more accurately read:

34

Thou wilt keep them (i.e., his words or the oppressed people), O LORD.
Thou wilt preserve us from this generation forever.

All the standard translations make both objects either "them"
or "us." We must try to determine what God inspired the
psalmist to say and then accurately render it. Three interpretations are possible: God will preserve the oppressed;
God will preserve those who believe in Him; God will keep
His word. Which one does the psalmist mean in this passage?
All are true.

PSALM 13

The question, "How long?" is typical of laments. Compare Psalms 6:3; 89:46; 90:13, and 94:3, 4. Psalm 13 has
this question four times in the first two verses.

In characteristic "trouble and trust" fashion, this psalm
begins with grievous lament and ends with genuine trust.
These six short verses move from despair to rejoicing, from
agony to ecstasy, from sorrow to song. Neither extreme is
insincere. Both are marked by integrity.

The psalmist is like most other believers; he often cannot
understand the ways of God. On the one hand, he knows
that God never forgets, but on the other hand, God apparently has forgotten him. God is supposed to be everywhere,
but at this critical intersection His location cannot be found.
God should be the psalmist's counsel and comfort yet he has
to find them in himself rather than in God. God is the Lord
of hosts and yet the present enemy is winning the victory.

All Scripture is profitable for something, according to
2 Timothy 3:16. The profit of these individual laments must

be in showing the modern saint that ancient saints had the same problems and questions. We are neither the first nor the last to wonder about God's sovereignty. David did it long ago.

In verses 3 and 4, the prayer changes from complaint to petition. See and do, Lord. Watch and act, my God. Consider and answer.

Verse 4 is the lever, noticed in other psalms, used to pry God into action with the threat that otherwise the adversary will be happy.

In the last two verses appears the declaration of trust. In spite of all he said before, the ancient writer asserts that he has trusted and that he will rejoice and sing. The bountiful dealings of God in the past outweigh any temporary discomfort. "Count your many blessings" is an appropriate commentary. Job lived out the details which this psalm only outlines in general terms. His testimony was, "Though he slay me, yet will I trust in him" (Job 13:15).

PSALM 14

Psalms 14 and 53 are nearly identical. The first three verses, which Paul echoes in Romans 3:10-12, have a familiar ring.

This is a wisdom psalm. The psalmist does not speak specifically of himself or of his people, except in the last verse. Personal pronouns are rarely found. The enemy, the fool, and the godly are mentioned in general terms.

Only a fool professes atheism (cf. Ps 10:4). The foolish atheist is also a wicked man. He is totally depraved in the theological sense. He can do nothing to please God. That which man might call righteousness is still sin in God's eyes. A sinner can do nothing but sin. God cannot find a single individual who seeks Him. No man comes to Christ except the Father draw him (Jn 6:44). This truth drives us harder to our knees. By His sovereign choice, we are in Christ and by that same sovereignty He must lead any others who come. There is none who seeks God, not even one.

In a certain sense the unregenerate man can know nothing rightly. Workers of iniquity have no knowledge, especially the saving knowledge of God. All ultimate truth evades them as long as God's Spirit is not in their hearts.

The victims of the godless man's violence are the people of God. Though the godless man does not call on God, he survives at the expense of God's people.

Verse 5 presents some questions. Who is in great fear? And where is *there?* The first answer might be that the people of God are in great fear, for they are the most immediate antecedents. But in the light of verse 6, it might rather be the evil men. They are afraid because they see that they cannot act with impunity against the righteous, for God is with them. Those wicked ones are addressed in verse 6. If the verb is taken as inceptive, as the Revised Standard Version does ("You would confound the plans of the poor"), the wicked are again seen as thwarted in their plan because God is the poor man's refuge.

The psalm ends with an invocation for God's salvation or deliverance. This anticipates the Messiah who would bring salvation to the elect of Israel when He comes to Zion. The name *Jesus* is from the Hebrew word for salvation, *yeshuah.* It is not necessary to understand this as an exilic psalm, for even in David's day, the captivity or bondage of sin prevailed. In a yet incompletely formed spiritual kingdom, the people were kept from rejoicing by the presence of so much wickedness. There are still people who deny God's existence and resist His Anointed, but someday the wicked will greatly tremble, while spiritual Israel will be glad.

Psalm 15 was probably used in the tabernacle liturgy. The first verse asks two questions: the remaining four verses answer them. It is one of the more practical psalms with down-to-earth applications.

Verse 1 is a lovely example of Hebrew parallelism. After the initial vocative, "LORD," each element has its companion in the second half. *Sojourn* and *dwell* are synonyms; *tabernacle* and *holy hill* are virtual synonyms.

This is a psalm of David, and the reference to the tabernacle may further indicate the period when the psalm was written. It may, however, merely indicate God's earthly dwelling place—His tent. "Who can be Your guest?" is a homey paraphrase.

The hill of God's holiness, to render the Hebrew more literally, is, of course, the central sanctuary of Israel at Jerusalem. The question is: What are the requirements for citizenship in Zion?

There are eleven parts to the answer and a summary line at the end. Each verse has three stichs or lines.

The first three statements have to do with integrity in general. The man who would enter God's house must be truthful. He must walk, work, and speak in truth and righteousness.

The next three (v. 3) deal with friends and neighbors. In particular, they have to do with evil talk. Gossip was a social ill then as it is now. For the most part, gossip concerns friends and neighbors, not foreign enemies. The candidate for worship must not have a vicious tongue that shames and berates his neighbor in front of others. It would prove interesting if we made these same simple requirements necessary for participation in our church worship!

Verse 4 details matters of religious attitude. The worshiper must hate what and whom God hates. Sin must not be tolerated (cf. Deu 7:5; 13:1-18; and Rev 2:20). Some say that the phrase "them that fear the LORD" is a technical designation for uncircumcised Gentiles who nevertheless were adherents to the God and religion of Israel. If that is so, the question is raised of tolerating Christians who are not completely orthodox. What should our attitude be toward those who differ? How widely can they differ? What is essential to cooperation? Are all who differ from us, even in the slightest, reprobate? Or are there some God-fearers outside our own ecclesiastical orbit?

The last stich of verse 4 points up in a most practical way how a man of integrity acts. Even if it costs him money, he keeps all his promises. He does not try to escape commitments. How many missionaries have suffered untold grief because people and churches who promised support defaulted? Such a weasel should not presume to be a welcome guest on God's holy hill.

Money is the subject of verse 5. Israelites were not to lend to their poor countrymen at interest (Ex 22:25). This is not, however, a prohibition of savings accounts or the stock market. Jesus Himself commended wise investors (Mt 25:14-27). Verse 5 condemns gross financial abuse of the poor. Bribing, the second matter, is also forbidden (cf. Ex 23:8).

The psalm could be summarized: If you do all the moral and spiritual positives, and avoid all the negatives, you will never be moved from fellowship with God.

PSALM 16

Michtam is in the title of six psalms: 16 and 56-60. No one knows for certain what it means, and in most versions it is simply transliterated.

Basically, this is a personal testimony to the blessedness in the Lord which the psalmist enjoys. At the outset there is a petition, and in the course of the poem there is an overtone of a polemic against other gods. There is some difficulty in the Hebrew which has given rise to the variety of renderings in verses 1-4.

The psalm does not fall easily into an outline; rather, the author moves from theme to theme, sometimes with obvious logical connection and sometimes without.

A prayer for perseverance opens the work followed immediately by the reason. The psalmist says, in effect, that God owes him deliverance because of his trust.

The subject changes in the difficult third verse. If the traditional rendering is accurate, the psalmist declares his delight in God's people as well as in God. Incidentally, the Hebrew words for the last phrase are *kal-hephsi-bam* ("in whom is all my delight"), essentially the same as *Hephzibah,* the new name God will give to His people, according to Isaiah 62:4.

The faithful worshiper of Yahweh (or Jehovah) makes his antipolytheistic punch felt in verse 4. He testifies that he has no part in giving gifts or drink offerings to anyone but the true God. In fact, he does not even use the names of other gods.

In contrast to the divided allegiances of other people, the psalmist's sole hope for inheritance is in the Lord. This idea of inheritance ties verse 6 to the preceding verses. The boundary lines for his property have fallen in such a way that all the land is fertile, watered, and productive. He has inherited no rocky mountainside, no barren desert, no sterile wasteland. He is examining his spiritual heritage in picture form. He is a blessed man.

Unlike many of us, this singer recognizes how prosperous and happy he is. Sole credit goes to God for His sage advice and welcome nocturnal promptings to praise. Do we use the opportunities afforded by sleepless nights to sing His praise?

All the sermons in the New Testament are replete with quotations from the Old. Peter's were no exception. In Acts 2:25-28 he quoted Psalm 16:8-10 and later in verse 31 identified verse 10 as Messianic. Paul, too, cited the tenth verse as he preached the resurrection of Christ to the people of Antioch of Pisidia (Acts 13:35).

These citations confirm for us the Messianic interpretation of this psalm. Not only can these statements describe David, but they describe Christ our Lord as well.

The testimony in verse 8b echoes the same word that is sounded at the close of Psalm 15. With our eyes on God and our hand in His, there is no greater safety. Because of all these blessings, David rejoices. *Glory* here means "soul" or "spirit." Verse 10 parallels *my soul* with *your faithful* or *holy one*.

Sheol is the Hebrew word for the place of the dead. It does not necessarily connote punishment as the English word *hell* does. To that place God would not and did not abandon His Messiah. The word parallel to *sheol* is perhaps best translated "corruption" (v. 10b). Christ did experience the pit, i.e., the grave, but not the attendant dissolution of His body (cf. Ac 2:31).

The psalm ends with a three-part verse affirming in positive terms that which verse 10 said in negative terms. God leads His chosen ones to the path of life—everlasting life. This narrow road, in turn, leads to all sorts of delights, which

41

are occasioned exclusively by the presence of God Himself. Compare the remarks on Psalm 11:7. The greatest prize of all is to see Christ and be like Him.

PSALM 17

The number of italicized words in the King James Version gives some indication of the difficulty in interpreting this psalm. All translators must make a number of guesses in order to provide a sensible English version.

Psalm 17 is a prayer. From beginning to end we witness the most agonized struggle of a man with his God. He needs protection. He needs assurance that he is in the right. He wants to see his enemies punished.

No neat outline fits this psalm. Several themes occur more than once, just as when we pray over a distressing problem and return again and again to it. Here is the psalmist's demand to be heard. It occurs in verse 1 and again in verses 2 and 6. "I am right" is another theme. It is in verses 1, 3, 4, and 5 (NASB). Specific prayer for protection appears in verses 7, 8, 9, 13, and 14. Verses 1b, 4b, 9, 10, 11, and 12 characterize the wicked. Verse 15 is a kind of testimony of hope.

Certain words and their synonyms occur again and again pointing to the unity of the work. *Cry, prayer, lips, mouth,* and *speech* belong in one group. *Ways, steps, paths,* and *feet* are roughly parallel. God is characterized by several anthropomorphisms. He has ears, a face, eyes, wings, hands, a sword, and a general bodily form, according to the last word of the poem.

Only five psalms are titled as prayers: 17, 86, 90, 102, and 142. Many more, however, are prayers. The word *prayer* actually occurs thirty-two times in the whole collection. No reason militates against the Davidic authorship of this psalm. A cursory reflection on the number of enemies he had gives ample substance to a prayer of this sort. Some enemies were foreign nations (e.g., the Philistines). Some were within Israel (e.g., Saul). Some were in his own family (e.g., Absalom). But his faithful ally was the God of Abraham, Isaac, and Jacob. The true disciple must expect enemies, perhaps even within his own household (Mt 10:36). But we, too, have that Friend who sticks closer than a brother (Pr 18:24).

The opening two verses introduce the prayer. Five pleading verbs are contained in this initial overture: *hear, attend, give ear, let,* and *look.* The word *right* or *righteous* stands without connection in the Hebrew of verse 1. Therefore it could be read: "Hear, O righteous Lord," or "Hear a righteous man," or "Hear what is right." In other words, the adjective could describe the Lord, the psalmist, or the prayer itself. The last is best because of the parallel "my cry."

His protestation of righteousness already appears in the first verse. Unlike his lying foes, his lips are free from deceit. In verses 3-5, that protestation of righteousness is elaborated on.

A legal tone permeates these opening verses, as revealed in such words as *right, sentence, equity, prove,* and *try.* The psalmist demands a hearing with the Judge of all men. He wants it because he knows he is right and the enemy is wrong. If God would only see that, then He would pay David damages and punish the enemies.

In verses 3 and following David reminds God that he has been proven and tried and found blameless. Even in the secret of night he asserts that God's all-knowing eyes have found in him nothing amiss. Neither his words nor his deeds

43

condemn him. On the other hand, the ways, work, and words of wicked men are violent.

Verse 6 concludes the first section, sounding again the notes of verse 1.

The psalm continues with a positive petition that God would demonstrate His *hesed*. This rich Hebrew word involves mercy, faithfulness to fulfill promises, and irrecovable covenant love. It is marvelous. The remainder of verse 7 is an elaborate description of God. The Hebrew is difficult and several translations are possible. The *New English Bible* has this fresh rendering:

> Show me how marvelous thy love can be,
>   who with thy hand does save
>   all who seek sanctuary from their enemies.

Because of the position of the words *your right hand* in Hebrew, it might better be understood that the enemies are "those who rebel against your right hand." The preposition can be either *by* or *against*.

In verses 9-12 the enemies from whom David pleads protection are described. They are wicked. They oppress him. They are deadly. They surround him. They are fat, i.e., greedy, and full of pride. They are boastful of their vicious accomplishments. They encircle the saint. They have their eyes set on his destruction. They are like ravenous lions lurking in secret, waiting to jump their innocent victim.

David implores God to arise and free him from all these terrors (v. 13). "Confront him to his face, cast him down but deliver me . . ." A series of *froms* marks this section: "from the wicked that oppress" (v. 9), "from the wicked" (v. 13), "from men" (v. 14), and "from men of the world" (v. 14).

The latter part of verse 14 is probably the most difficult part of the psalm to understand. Most interpreters take it as a description of the wicked and of his rewards, which are only temporal. Maybe David has his tongue in his cheek. The enemy, the man whose god is his belly, can only hope for transitory fortune, but God has "treasured up" for him only punishment.

In striking contrast is the hope of the believer. He, either figuratively in this present life or in reality in the next, will see God's face and behold His form. That is the only satisfaction he wants, for he knows that the righteous alone inherit that reward. Let the wicked have the cursed wealth of this condemned world. We shall see the King some day!

PSALM 18

What a beautiful way to begin a psalm! "I love you, LORD." And why not, since God was to David and did for him the dozens of things spelled out in the following fifty verses?

There is no reason to doubt the accuracy of the title to this, the fourth longest poem in the Psalter. Second Samuel 22:1-51 duplicates both the title and the psalm itself with minor variations. In that historical book is a kind of summary of David's life. Saul was now dead. Absalom was dead. The Philistines were subdued. David's kingdom was relatively secure.

A broad outline might be:

A praise introduction (1-3)
A picture of God the deliverer (4-19)
The basis of that deliverance (20-30)
Testimony of victory through God (31-45)
A praise benediction (46-50)

The opening three verses praise God in very general terms. He is the writer's strength, rock, fortress, deliverer, shield, horn of salvation, and high tower. All of these have to do with the military; in fact, the whole psalm has a strong militaristic ring. Those over whom David triumphed were military foes.

Beginning with verse 4 and continuing through verse 6, David describes his deliverance, as it were, from death. *Saul* and *Sheol* have the same consonants in Hebrew; only the vowels are different. Because of this, some want to substitute *Sheol* for *Saul* in the title. *Sheol* is parallel with death here in verse 5.

Jonah knew this psalm and referred to verses 4-6 in his second chapter. The reference to "temple" in poetry does not prove that the poem is post-Davidic. This word is used in connection with the boyhood of Samuel many years before Psalm 18 was written (1 Sa 1:9, 3:3).

Verses 7-15 contain an extended theophany. The earth and the foundations of the mountains shook, trembled, and quaked because God was angry. There is no record of an earthquake accompanying any of David's deliverances. All this may be a highly figurative description of the thundering army of the Lord of hosts.

The descriptions in verse 8 sound like a volcanic eruption but perhaps are only a thunder and lightning storm, as verses 13-14 indicate. Whatever its exact meteorlogical nature, this violent storm is evidence of God's vindicating, punishing power. The resultant flood from excess rain and melted hail washes bare the bedrock of the land (v. 15). The blast of the breath of God's nostrils is, of course, the wind.

The personal pronoun *me* appears again in verse 17. By all these natural and supernatural means God saves His saint from the hateful enemy. Even though they choose to attack David when he is down, thus multiplying his calamity, God chooses to bring him to safety. The *wide place* is in contrast to the narrow escape, the tight situation, the squeeze the enemy put on him.

It is an easy transition to the next point in the outline. The basis of God's deliverance is already indicated in verses 18-19, and 20-30 only elaborate on it. Simply put, the reason God saved David is that "he delighted in him." That answer sounds too simple to many unbelievers. Rather than believe Christ and win eternal life, they espouse a more difficult religion of works which brings no salvation at all.

Some might accuse David of arrogance and proud self-righteousness. But remember that ultimate righteousness comes from trusting God. This one "good deed" of belief in God's saving provision and forgiving power is counted by God to outweigh all sin.

Ten times over David tells why God dealt so generously with him. All of this is based on the one little statement in verse 19: "Because He delighted in me." If God chooses to be for us, none can stand against us (Ro 8:31). We are His by sovereign election and He cannot forsake us. David was not saved by works—only by *the* work of faith (cf. Jn 6:29).

Verses 25-26 contain an interesting little series. God is what we are to Him. The good think He is good. The bad think He is bad. If we confess Christ before men, He will confess us before the Father. If we deny Him before men, He will deny us before the Father (Mt 10:32-33).

In David's day, as well as in Peter's and in ours, God exalts the humble but humiliates the proud (1 Pe 5:5). With the figures of a lamp and a shield, the psalmist concludes this section. Verse 29b is one of this writer's favorite testimony verses. It comes to mind whenever a human impossibility is faced. "By my God I can leap over a wall!"

47

Joshua and the people of Israel did it literally at Jericho. David and his army did it at Jerusalem. Why can't we?

The next large section (vv. 31-45) relates in glowing terms just how Yahweh, the only true God, gave David victory over his numerous antagonists. In figurative terms, God clothed him with strength and made his way perfect; that is, He completely prepared David. God made his feet like deer's feet, his bow like brass, and gave him the shield of salvation. (Compare verses 32, 34-35, 39 with Eph 6:13-17). Having so armed His king, God held his right hand and let him take giant strides, while not letting his foot slip. Thus he chased the enemy, stabbed them, and had them fall at his feet. Notice the typical Semitic repetition in verses 37-42. How many times and in how many ways does he repeat the fact of their annihilation?

From what seem to be local triumphs, the psalmist turns, in verse 43, to boast of the international fame that God granted him. Perhaps the first stich of verse 43 indicates that internal factions had ceased. He had consolidated all areas of Israel. In the balance of the verse the annexation of nations is the subject. For all this, the only credit he takes is that he trusted God. God gave the deliverances and deserves all the praise.

The last five verses of the poem are a benediction and summarize briefly all that was said above. The ideas of rock and salvation (v. 46) echo verse 2 in the laudatory introduction. The victories recited in verses 47 and 48 reflect the bulk of the central part of the work. The last two verses conclude both the benediction and the psalm.

Notice the evangelistic emphasis of this ancient, godly king. He declares that he will give thanks "among the nations"; that is, he will tell these recently conquered peoples of the greatness of his God. Why should such a man of faith not be concerned that his subjects, as well, know the true God?

Verse 50 has the word *messiah* in it (*anointed* in KJV). The phrases "to his king," "to his anointed," "to David," and "to his seed" are parallel. That seed, we learn elsewhere, is none other than Christ our Lord.

To a certain extent we can share in the exultation of this psalm. Not only might we slightly resemble David in our faith, but because we are in Christ we share in His conquests as He builds and blesses His Kingdom.

PSALM 19

Psalm 19 is a favorite psalm of many people. It is very clear in its arrangement and simple in its message. The author speaks of God's revelation in nature and in the Bible. Here is a three-point outline:

The World of God (1-6)
The Word of God (7-10)
The Way of God (11-14)

Men learn of God from the realm of nature, but more specifically from His written revelation. With the coming of Christ in the fullness of time the world received God's living Word (Jn 1:1).

The device of parallelism is apparent throughout this psalm. The first verse is a clear example of it. *Heaven* and the *firmament* (expanse or vault) are the two subjects, *declare* and *show* are the verbs, and *the glory of God* and *His handiwork* are the objects. A Bible student could profitably examine this entire psalm in the light of parallelism.

That God is evident in nature is believed by all except the

most hardened of those who resist Him. Numerous and eloquent are the poems of men to this effect. Sunsets, seashores, starry nights, trees, flowers, waterfalls—all are the subjects men write about.

> Poems are made by fools like me,
> But only God can make a tree.

These famous words of Joyce Kilmer do just what the opening part of this psalm does: present the Creator through nature.

Verse 2 declares that night and day alike provide evidence of God's existence. The word rendered *uttereth* (KJV) has the sense of "gush" or "surge" behind it in the original language. Having spoken of a universal speech, the psalmist continues by saying that it is never heard. The word *where* does not appear in Hebrew, so what we have are three negative statements. "There is no speech." "There is no language." "Their voice is not heard." The first two-thirds of verse 4 complete this thought. The unheard speech, the words or message, is everywhere—to the ends of the earth. *Line,* which might be slang in our language, is not such in Hebrew. (Paul quotes the Greek translation of the Old Testament in Romans 10:18, which reads, "their voice" in the NASB.) The hymn, "The Spacious Firmament," by Joseph Addison is a beautiful commentary on these verses. Here is just one of the stanzas:

> What though, in solemn silence, all
>   Move round this dark terrestrial ball?
> What though no real voice nor sound
>   Amid the radiant orbs be found?
> In reason's ear they all rejoice,
>   And utter forth a glorious voice,
> Forever singing as they shine,
>   "The hand that made us is divine."

50

To depict the worldwide communication of God's existence and glory, the psalmist chooses the sun's daily coverage of the earth. This picture continues through verse 6. But verse 5 is an illustration of an illustration. Evidence for God is like the sun. The sun, in turn, is like a bridegroom or a ready runner. These were the most glorious specimens the writer could use to characterize the beauty and strength of the sun. In its orbit it begins at one horizon, makes what appears from our perspective to be a high half circle, and goes to the other horizon. Everything derives warmth from it; all energy comes from it—a scientific truth recognized only in modern times.

Verses 7-10 speak of the Bible. Here are six synonyms for the Word: *law, testimony, precepts, commandments, fear,* and *ordinances.* Then there are the descriptive adjectives: *perfect, sure, right, pure, clean,* and the additional ones in verse 9, *true* and *righteous altogether.* Following each of the first five adjectives is a statement of what the Word of God does. It restores or converts the soul. It makes the simple wise. It rejoices the heart. It enlightens the eyes. It endures forever. An interesting study would be to rearrange the three elements of each of these strophes. There are more than fifteen possible combinations.

Notice in verse 7a that the first thing which the Word of God does is to restore the soul. This word can also be translated *converting* (KJV). The priority given to this word is intentional. Before we can be wise, before the heart really rejoices, before our eyes can be clearly enlightened, and before we find the Bible more precious than gold and sweeter than honey, we must be saved. Conversion is the first step.

The gold and the honey of verse 10 easily prompt many analogies. Like gold, the Bible is priceless. The Bible is the most valuable of all books. The Bible is enduring. The Bible serves as a standard. Like honey the Bible is sweet.

The Bible is nourishing. The Bible has healing qualities. The Bible admits of no impurities.

The last four verses of the psalm tell us what the Bible does—what the way of God is. The writer, who calls himself a servant, testifies that there are to be found in the Bible both warning and reward—a hell to shun and a heaven to win.

Study of the Bible moves us to a consciousness of sin and to a sensitivity for holiness. Such is the gist of the prayer which continues to the end of the psalm. David knows that pride (presumption) can be the most deceiving of all sin, so he prays for cleansing from it. The sister of pride is hypocrisy; hence the petition in the last verse of the psalm that his thoughts might correspond to his words. When Christ rules our minds, and our words speak His mind, we will not have to worry. Paul urges us in 2 Corinthians 10:5b to bring into captivity every thought to the obedience of Christ.

PSALM 20

All the verbs of the first half of Psalm 20 can be rendered two ways. For example, the first line can read, "The LORD hear you" or "The LORD will hear you." In grammatical terms the first form is a jussive and the second a simple future. In Hebrew they often cannot be distinguished. The difference in the total interpretation of the psalm is that it is either a prayer or a prediction. Most standard translations opt for the former.

Essentially, this is a prayer *for* David. The problems then arise: Did David write it or did someone write it about him? The word translated *of* could as well mean *for* or *concerning*.

Assuming that the prayer is for King David, the psalm is a beautiful expression by a devoted subject. With slight modification, parts of this prayer could be adapted for our own political leaders.

The first three verses are an uninterrupted series of petitions. Notice the interesting parallel in verse 1 of "The Lord" with "the name of the God of Jacob." His name is Himself. Even in the New Testament, the idea persists that the person is the name. So we are urged to call on the name of the Lord, believe in the name of Christ (Jn 1:12), and pray in Jesus' name (Jn 14:13). *Name* occurs again in verses 5 and 7.

A *selah* appears at the end of verse 3 but the reason is unknown. It concludes two verses which speak of liturgy, but it is not a major break in the prayer.

The fourth verse continues in the form of a prayer wish. The desire of the heart of the godly man should correspond to the desire of the heart of God (Ps 37:4). When we delight in the Lord, He will delight in us and give us what we want. When we are near God, we want what He wants. Jesus said essentially the same thing in the Sermon on the Mount: "Seek ye first the kingdom of God, and his righteousness; and all these things shall be added unto you" (Mt 6:33).

Verse 5 is a transition. Here first person pronouns appear and continue to the end of the psalm. The Revised Standard Version continues the form of the verbs as in the previous verses, understanding them as cohortatives: "May we rejoice," "May the Lord fulfil."

Verse 5 is also the last verse of the prayer. Verses 6-8 are a testimony. Anticipating a response the psalmist with conviction affirms his knowledge of God's salvation. The

53

"anointed" (Heb. *messiah*) is David in this context, but a Messianic allusion cannot be ruled out.

The word *trust,* or *boast,* (v. 7) does not appear in the Hebrew, but is clearly implied by the parallel line. Zechariah 4:6 echoes the sentiment of this verse: "Not by might, nor by power, but by my spirit, saith the LORD of hosts."

In America it is very easy to trust something or someone other than the Lord. Our economic bliss gives us a false feeling of security and independence. Often, it is only in times of crisis that we are cornered into trusting God. Perhaps we should pray for more "heat and pressure" on our faith in order to produce more holiness and piety. Then we will witness the unbelievers' bowing, not to us as their conquerors but to Christ, their newly claimed King. This is the reason we stand upright (v. 8).

The concluding verse is another prayer. The plea, "save," is "Hosanna" used on Palm Sunday.

But who is the king? (v. 9). Though some modern translations take David to be the king, the Hebrew has it parallel with the Lord. That means that ultimately the prayer is not that King David, but the King of kings Himself, should save us.

PSALM 21

Psalm 21 falls easily into two main parts. The division is between verses 7 and 8. The first half expresses the king's gratitude for blessings. The second half describes God's overthrow of the enemy. The first and last verses are complementary. The phrase "in your strength" appears in both. In the first verse the king rejoices in God. In the last verse we, the worshipers, sing and praise His power. The psalm was probably used in the divine services in Jerusalem.

After the introductory verse stating that the king does rejoice, the ensuing six verses tell why. God gave him his heart's desire. (Compare the commentary on Psalm 20:4.) God answered his prayer. He crowned the king with a golden crown and let him have a long life.

But the thing in which the king gloried most was God's salvation (v. 5). The writer may have had a military victory in mind, or the higher, ultimate purpose of God's deliverance, that is, eternal life. We ought to enjoy temporal blessings but also to remember that the source of greatest joy should come from our hope of everlasting life.

As in verses 6-7 of Psalm 20, verse 7 of this psalm points up the king's trust in God's never-failing, covenant love. Only as he trusts will he not be moved, regardless of the foes who stand against him.

A contrast begins with verse 8. Whereas in the first half positive words abound—blessings, goodness, life, glory, salvation, honor, majesty, trust, and lovingkindness—now negative words are abundant. In verses 8-12, these terms color the picture: *enemies, hate, anger, wrath, destroy,* and *evil.*

This second half of Psalm 21 describes God's dealing with the enemy. In verse 8 He finds out who they are. The punishment begins in verse 9. *Anger* and *wrath* poetically relate the first two stichs of verse 9 to each other; *swallow* and *devour* relate the second and third stichs; while *fire* occurs in the first and third.

Verses 10-11 show God frustrating the selfish human hopes and dastardly designs of the enemy. The heirs who would enjoy their fathers' ill-gotten wealth are destroyed. They are caught in their own traps. Their bows literally backfire; they shoot themselves. That is the lot of the godless. All this gave the ancient Israelites great comfort and a basis for praise. They blessed God who had destroyed their enemies.

The last verse wraps up these sentiments. *We,* the worshipers of the true God, who make the Lord our strength, will sing of and praise God's power.

PSALM 22

The word *Messiah* (Christ) does not occur in Psalm 22, yet no other psalm speaks so specifically of our Lord Jesus Christ and His passion. The opening phrase was the cry of the Saviour while He hung on the cross. The vile taunt of verse 8 was on the lips of the thoughtless crowd around Calvary. Three gospel writers cited verse 18 when the soldiers gambled for His robe. And the author of Hebrews (2:12) quotes verse 22 and applies it to Christ.

In the title, *Aijeleth ha-shahar* (Heb.; cf. NASB) may be translated as "deer of the morning," probably the name of the tune to which this psalm was sung.

Verses 1-21 constitute a prayer of the righteous sufferer; 22-25 are praise; 26-31 are a prediction.

Within the first twenty-one verses, the sufferer goes from complaint to trust and back again several times. Verses 1-2, 6-8, and 12-18 are complaints. Verses 3-5, 9-11, and 19-21 are prayers of trust.

The *Eli, Eli, lama sabachthani* of Matthew 27:46 is the Aramaic of Psalm 22:12. This expression is the traditional fourth word from the cross. When the Son of God uttered these words, the greatest transaction of all time occurred. The Righteous died for the guilty. The guiltless One bore the sin of many. The "many" need only believe and live. We live because He died.

The opening words could apply to David only in a hyperbolic way. That which could apply to him only by way of comparison applies to Christ quite specifically. Yet even the *bulls* of verse 12 must be understood figuratively. Neither David nor Christ was literally surrounded by angry bulls.

The complaint continues in verse 2. Night and day witness the sufferer's plea for a hearing.

Beginning with verse 3, the psalmist turns to an argument from history. He reminds God of His past faithfulness and former deliverances and attempts to force Him to act. Sometimes such a tack is for the benefit of the one praying. We sometimes forget that God is altogether good, that He cannot deny Himself, and that He does nothing except for our welfare. A brief reflection on our spiritual pilgrimage can be most helpful and therapeutic.

Verse 6 again takes up the complaint. The agonizing saint says he is the lowest of all animals. He is far below human status. He is a worm and, as such, is despised by all.

Shooting out the lip is like sticking out the tongue or razzing. Both Matthew (27:39) and Mark (15:29) report on the wagging heads of the bewildered onlookers. But the more vile of Christ's enemies gave vent with the seething taunt: "Let God save him." These words faintly echo those of Satan during the temptation in the wilderness (Mt 4:6).

In verse 9 the pendulum swings back the other way again. Once more the psalmist reflects on God's former mercies. From birth until now he has seen only love and concern. Now that trouble besets him he prays that God will be near to help (v. 11). The author is not a foxhole convert; he is not a crisis Christian. He is a well-established believer with experience in prayer and faith. He has seen God work in the past.

The long, descriptive complaint of verses 12-18 contains many direct and indirect allusions to the events of Passion Week. The Bashan bulls represent the established religion of Judaism and the powerful Roman government. For years they had surrounded Christ waiting for the opportunity to "gore" Him. As a hungry, salivating lion they lurked in secret to take Him. And now they have Him on a cross—dehydrated and hungry, seemingly helpless and hopeless. But note that it is God, not the enemy, who has brought the sufferer to death. Still He acknowledges God's sovereignty. Still He sees Himself as part of the divine plan of the ages. Though dogs and evildoers nail His hands and feet, though soldiers crucify Him at the command of the government and the urging of the maddened throng incited to hate by the Jewish leaders, yet it is God His Father who brings Him to the dust of death (v. 15b). That is the key verse in this psalm; it is one of the essential doctrines of the Christian faith. God *willed* that Christ should die.

Some Bible students see many more details in these verses. For instance, the reference to water might be connected with the piercing of the Saviour's side. Blood and water poured out of that laceration (Jn 19:34). The bones being out of joint may refer to the fact that Christ's bones were not broken (Jn 19:33), only out of joint because of the hanging.

Verses 19-21 are the last in the prayer cycle. Some of the animals named above reappear in this prayer. The word *darling* (KJV) of verse 20 is interesting. It is built on the word *one* or *together* and probably has reference to the composite person—body and soul.

The psalmist asserts that he will praise God (v. 22). Then he adjures his audience to praise Him (v. 23). Apparently the prayers of the first half of the psalm were answered, at least the eye of faith saw the answers, for the content of the praise is in verse 24. God did not ignore the afflicted. He did not hide His face but listened and answered.

With the praise went vows (v. 25). The inspired author probably vowed to tell others faithfully of his deliverance. He promised to testify of God's keeping power.

The concluding six verses are primarily in the future tense and sound like predictions. Since God has heard, the meek shall eat and be satsified. Then all the remote parts of the world will learn and turn to the Lord. The kingdoms of this world will become the kingdom of our Lord and of His Christ (cf. v. 28; Rev 11:15). The rich and the poor, the living and the dead will all eventually bow. Generation after generation will recite the deeds of the Lord. People not then yet born would learn what Christ would do and has done.

PSALM 23

The Twenty-third Psalm is the favorite of millions. No other psalm comes close to its popularity. There are dozens of translations, paraphrases, and hymn arrangements.

The psalm is basically a testimony of great faith. The first four verses use pictures from the pastoral life that David led before he was engaged by Saul for palace service. The fifth and sixth verses have multiple metaphors.

With brief strokes the picture takes shape. First there is a shepherd, who is the Lord. Then there is a satisfied sheep, the psalmist. The pasture is green and the stream trickles through it. It is a beautiful picture of the believer and his Lord. Jesus used the illustration of sheep and shepherds many times (e.g., Mt 7:15; 18:12f.; 25:32f.; Jn 10:2ff.).

Sheep are among the most helpless and stupid of animals.

They desperately need guidance and assistance. Probably for this reason God's people are likened to them.

Verse 3 gives an interpretation of verse 2. As sheep's appetites are satisfied with ample grass and abundant water, so God restores the soul of the spiritually fatigued. The verb *restores* might be translated "converts," which would load the psalm with additional theological meaning. The *leading* by still waters of verse 2 is paralleled by the leading in righteousness of verse 3. For His own sake He leads us to do right. If we sin we offend Him and tarnish His reputation. So, for the sake of His own name, as well as for our good, He points us in the right direction.

Verse 4 again takes up the figure of shepherding. The famous opening phrase can be translated either "shadow of death" or "deep darkness." The latter should not detract, however, from the use of the psalm in connection with death. The sheep should never fear, whether it be light or dark, whether it lives or dies. Two trusty implements are in the shepherd's hand. One is a club for beating off the enemies of the sheep, the other is a stick for nudging the sheep along. God both defends and directs the believer. He protects him and points out the way. The mere knowledge that the shepherd has these two instruments comforts the flock.

The metaphor of verse 5 is that of a banqueting victor. It may have been the practices in ancient times for the winner to feast in front of the starving prisoners of war (cf. Judg 1:7). Anointing or perfuming of the banquet guests was a gracious gesture by the host. When the guests were prepared to dine, their cup was filled to overflowing. These three pictures—the table, the oil, and the cup—all typify God's provision for His people. The table may be the Lord's Supper; the oil, the filling of the Holy Spirit; and the cup, the daily benefits with which God loads His people.

The last verse is more than a picture. In truth, God has a

"house" in which believers will live eternally. Otherwise Jesus would not have told us so (Jn 14:2). God's goodness and covenant faithfulness will accompany us not only in this life but in the life to come.

It may have been David's hope to live, while on earth, at the temple which he wished to build, but his eternal hope was to be where God would be, in heaven. Three possibilities exist for translating verse 6b. The well-known "I shall dwell" is one. "I shall rest" is a second. "I shall return to" is a third. All of these suggestions are grammatically, exegetically, and theologically possible. It is clear that David anticipated being forever where God is.

PSALM 24

Psalm 24 was doubtlessly a liturgical hymn. The question-anwer motif in verses 3-5, 8, and 10 indicates that the psalm was probably sung antiphonally. One choir or soloist asked the questions and another responded.

The psalm is in three parts. Verses 1-2 express in grand and cosmic terms the extent of God's domain. Verses 3-6 are an examination for participation in the worship at Jerusalem. This section is reminiscent of Psalm 15. The third section is verses 7-10, and sounds like a triumphal march.

Verse 1 declares that God owns everything. Verse 2 states that He made everything. In more modern language, "The earth is the Lord's and everything that fills it." The parallel to *earth* is *world* and to *fulness* is *they that inhabit it*. In other words, everything and everybody belong to God.

With verse 3 begins the liturgical examination. Who may go and stand in the sanctuary? Four stipulations are found in verse 4. First, the would-be worshiper must have clean hands—a symbol of a clean and faultless life. Second, he must have a pure heart—a symbol of a right attitude. Third, he must not have lifted his soul to vanity, meaning that he does not have an appetite for foolishness. Fourth, he must not swear deceitfully; that is, he must be a man who keeps his word and pays his bills. In general terms these two positive and two negative requirements cover most of life.

The man who passes these tests is the man whom the Lord will bless and admit into His presence. He is a member of the generation which seeks God. *Generation* (v. 6) here means family, species, or kind. *O Jacob* is elliptical for *O God of Jacob*.

Verses 7-10 may have been sung when the ark was brought to Jerusalem (cf. 2 Sa 6:12ff.). This anthem may also foreshadow both the Messiah's coming to Jerusalem on Palm Sunday and His victorious reentry into the Father's presence at the ascension. Verses 7 and 9 are identical, verses 8 and 10 are almost identical. The two *selahs* in this psalm are appropriately placed at the ends of major divisions, but no indication of their meaning is apparent.

PSALM 25

The author of Psalm 25 employed two fascinating literary devices. The psalm is an alphabetic acrostic. It is also an elaborate chiasmus.

Every verse, with only minor exceptions, begins with each successive letter of the Hebrew alphabet. In the second verse only the second word begins with the second letter of the alphabet. Verse 5 must be divided in half and assigned two letters. Verse 18 should begin with a *qoph* instead of a *resh,* as does verse 19. Verse 22 is beyond the end of the alphabet. Here is the chiastic outline:

```
 1   A  "I lift up my soul unto them"
 2      B  "Let not shame"
 3         C  Treacherous shamed
 4-5a         D  Three petitions for guidance
 5b             E  Psalmist's salvation
 5c                F  "I wait"
 6                   G.1  God's mercy
 7                      G.2  God's goodness implored
 8-9                       H  God's instruction of the meek
 10a                          I  God's faithfulness
 10b                            I'  The faithful
 11                               J  "Pardon me"
 12-13                          H'  Instruction of God-fearers
 14-15                       G.1'  God's friendship and covenant
 16a                      G.2'  "Have mercy"
 16b                   F'  "I am desolate"
 17a               E'  Psalmist's troubles
 17b-19a        D'  Three petitions for salvation
 19b         C'  Psalmist's enemies
 20      B'  "Let not shame"
 21   A'  "I wait for thee"
 22                               J'  "Redeem Israel"
```

Such an elaborate arrangement could not have been acci-
dental. Perhaps this was an aid to memory just as the acrostic feature was. But imagine the ingenuity of the poet who
put this together with these two features intermingled and
still produced such a meaningful psalm!

A third, less rigid device also marks this work. Many of
the verses are linked by key words. A verse may pick up
a word from its preceding verse and be connected to the
following with yet a different word. This is how it works:
Verses 1-2 are connected by the first person singular tes-

timonies, "I lift up" and "I have trusted." Verses 2-3 are connected by the idea of *shame*. *Teach me* occurs in both verses 4-5. *Remember* appears in 6-7. In verse 7 we read of God's goodness and in verse 8 that He is good. The word *way* links verses 8-9. The pattern continues, with irregularity, through this and many other psalms. This feature is part of the Semitic thought pattern. Even the apostle Paul often used it in his epistles (e.g., 2 Th 1:3-10).

There is a simpler outline to this prayer which is based on the use of pronouns and other features of the content. Verses 1-7 are petitions of the psalmist. Verses 8-10 are statements about God's character and deeds. Verse 11 is like a parenthesis, as seen in the chiastic outline. It also marks the halfway point. Verses 12-14 contain more statements about God's deeds. Verses 15-21 revert to the petition form. Verse 22 is a kind of summary, communal petition (as verse 11 was a personal petition) marking the end of the second half of the psalm.

The prayer is very personal, yet the subject matter is very general. Both the nature of the enemy's oppression and the character of the deliverance sought are universally applicable. For this reason some think this is a liturgical psalm fitted for any number of occasions.

The first verse is a statement of faith. But from verses 2-7 a series of imperative verbs forms the content of the prayer. The first four petitions, those in verses 2-3, are negative: "Let me not . . . Let not my enemies . . . Let none that wait . . . Let them be ashamed. . . ." Then follows a series of positive imperatives: "Show me . . . teach me . . . guide me . . . teach me. . . ."

Verses 6-7 are marked by *remember* and *don't remember*. On the one hand, the prayer is that God would remember His mercy and His commitment to love. *Hesed*

64

(see notes on Ps 17:7) appears a second time in the middle of verse 7. On the other hand, the prayer is that God would forget the petitioner's sins and transgressions. Within verses 6-7 is a simple chiasmus.

> Remember your mercy.
> Remember not my sins.
> Remember me according to your mercy.

Verses 8-14 (with the exception of verse 11) provide additional bases for a man coming to God in prayer. God is good and upright. He does instruct, guide, and teach. Verses 8-9 have some of the same words used in the prayer of verses 4-5. Verse 10 teaches that all that God does for those who fear Him is based on His consistent, faithful love and truth. The estate of such a man blessed by God is portrayed in verses 12-14.

In verse 15 the first person pronouns again appear and in verse 16 imperative verbs once more set the style. Because of the faith asseverated in verse 15, the psalmist is bold to pray as he does in the following verses. "Turn and have mercy." "Bring me out." "Consider my affliction." "Forgive my sins." "Consider my enemy." "Keep and deliver me." "Let me not be shamed." "Let integrity preserve me." Note the identical word *consider* (*look* in KJV, v. 18) which begins verses 18-19. He prays: "Consider me and consider my enemies."

The psalm concludes with a general prayer for Israel's redemption. If the psalm is a communal prayer, then this seems to be a fine summary and benediction. All the individual petitions can be wrapped up in the one word, *redeem*. And all the people and problems they need deliverance from can be wrapped up in the word *troubles*. The complement to this last verse is verse 11, where the psalmist uses the argument, "For thy name's sake." All deliverance, all redemption, and all salvation are for His glory and our good. By these mighty acts His name is honored.

PSALM 26

Psalm 26 is classed as an individual lament. In this psalm David demands of God a hearing so that he may be vindicated. The first two verses are his demand. The third through the eighth verses are his protestations of innocence and righteousness. Verses 9-12 contain a mixture of petition, promise, and testimony.

Four imperative verbs make up the appeal for justice in verses 1-2. In verse 1 the plaintiff is convinced of his integrity—a theme he expands in verses 3-8. He swears that he has walked in uprightness and has trusted. His is not a plea for forgiveness but a demand for divine exoneration. The older word *reins* (v. 2, KJV) in newer translations is *mind* or the like. The ancient seat of the emotions was thought to be in the lower torso.

The protestation of integrity in verses 3-8 contains testimony to the avoidance of sins of both omission and commission. The psalmist did walk in truth. How can a man expect to place a claim with God if he is not a man of truth? He did not sit with men of falsehood. How can God's people expect to entertain successfully both right and wrong? He loved God's house. Why should we go if we do not? He hated the assembly of evildoers. Who, today, are the companions of God's people Monday through Saturday?

Having disclaimed in verses 4-5 any evil associations, David relates his going undefiled to the sanctuary. Washed hands symbolize a sinless life. Then, in general terms, he promises to relate all God's wonderful works.

The third section of the psalm contains more petitions, but it also reflects the testimony and promise features of verses 3-8. The requests are *gather not* (v. 9) and *redeem me and be merciful* (v. 11). Verse 10 is a relative clause describing wicked men among whom he does not want to be counted. They are men of blood, that is, murderers. They take bribes. But the psalmist walks in integrity. He stands on level ground (v. 12). That phrase may be understood several ways. He is a man "on the level," so to speak or he dares to approach the Lord on the same level or he is in a position where he cannot fall. The phrase may be in contrast to the last phrase in verse 1 which, in the King James Version, is rendered, "I shall not slide."

As with other psalms, David concludes this one as if God had already answered his requests. Because of those unrecorded answers he declares that he will bless the Lord in the congregation. Sometimes God's people are long on asking and short on thanking and blessing. Even if we do not receive an immediate answer, shouldn't we bless God nonetheless?

PSALM 27

This psalm of David focuses on that ancient king's fearless trust in God. He trusts his God for strength (vv. 1, 14), for safety (vv. 2, 3, 12, 13), for instruction (vv. 4, 11), for salvation (vv. 1, 9), and for answered prayer (vv. 7-10). Sometimes the psalm is outlined simply as David's testimony (vv. 1-6) and his prayer (vv. 7-14). But it is interesting that much testimony is also reflected in the prayer.

According to verse 1, the Lord is light, salvation and

strength. Therefore the believer has no cause to fear. Perhaps these three things refer to the three elements of our person. He is light for our otherwise darkened minds. He is salvation for our otherwise lost souls. He is strength for our otherwise weak bodies (cf. Is 40:31).

David testifies, in verses 2-3, of deliverance from adversaries, and prays for a continuation of the same in verse 12. Other psalms record the inhospitality and outright hatred he had for his enemies. He resisted them because they were the enemies of Israel and of God.

The deepest desire of the king's heart is exposed in verse 4. He wants to be near God, where it is beautiful, where his inquiries can be answered, where it is safe. We may seek the Lord wherever He is found, and that is everywhere. We may call on Him when He is near, and that is all the time. Here David prays to be in God's house all his days, while in Psalm 23:6 he prays to be there for eternity.

Some question may arise regarding the reference to the temple, which was not built in David's lifetime. It seems that he was searching for a word to parallel "house" and "tabernacle," even though *the* temple had not yet been built. On the other hand, he may have had his eye on the heavenly temple, the life after death when such a privilege would be available to him.

The latter part of verse 5 contains a precious picture. The writer hopes for a tent (tabernacle) to shelter him. God is such. David hopes for a solid rock on which to stand. And God is such also.

Verse 6 summarizes the psalmist's testimony. It mentions deliverance from enemies. It mentions his joyous activity in the tabernacle. And it mentions the purpose for it all—to give glory to God.

The seventh verse begins the prayer proper. This section, too, has some fascinating interplays with words. Notice how each successive verse is connected to the preceding one by a catchword. The word "face" connects verses 8 and 9, and the word "forsake" connects verses 9 and 10. By saying his parents have forsaken him, he probably means that they have died.

The matter of enemies and adversaries occurs toward the end of the prayer even as it occurred near the beginning of the testimony. The *plain path* (KJV) of verse 11 might better be translated "straight" or "righteous." As Christians we must have impeccable lives before those who are enemies of the cross. To lead such sterling lives would be impossible if it were not for Him who lives in us and for the hope which lies before us. Unless we had believed to see the goodness of the Lord in the land of the living (v. 13), we would have no hope of eternal life or purpose for this one.

At the very conclusion of the psalm is a timely word for us. Incidentally it is in chiastic arrangement:

> Wait on the LORD.
>   Be strong.
>   Let thy heart take courage.
> Wait on the LORD.

PSALM 28

Typical of the personal laments is Psalm 28. It evidences a common outline:

> Invocation (1-2)
> Imprecation (3-5)
> Intercession and praise (6-9)

God is addressed in verse 1 as "my rock." This appellative, rock, is found sprinkled throughout the Old Testament (Deu

69

32:4, 15, 18, 30, 31; Ps 18:2, 31; 19:14; *et al.*). Perhaps this is a subtle reference to Christ (cf. Mt 16:18; 1 Co 10:4).

The *lest* (v. 1) is the "lever" David uses on God to move Him to act. He asks God if He is willing to let His servant go to the grave unrewarded and unvindicated. In verse 2 he begs that the sound of his supplications be heard as he raises his hands toward the holy of holies. The English word *oracle* correctly translates the Hebrew *debir*. That root means *to speak*. This word and the Holy of Holies are put together in 1 Kings 6:16, 19. No one but the high priest, and he but once a year, actually entered that sacred inner room, but both layman and priest prayed facing it. God dwelt in that holy place in a special way. Here David lifts his hands toward it in a gesture of unfeigned desperation.

The content of the supplication is in verses 3-5. Mostly it is a plea for the punishment of the wicked. Such curses are called "imprecations." Verse 3 details the nature of evil men. They are insincere, saying one thing but doing another. They greet a neighbor with *"shalom"* (peace), but plot his downfall in their minds.

Verse 4 is the essence of the curse. Basically David prays, "Do to them what they have done to others." Their sinful ways are the result of ignoring God. This is the diagnosis of every sinner's problem—he does not know God. He has not heard or does not believe that God is, and that He is a just and holy God. In the end He will break down and not build up those who choose to be His enemies. These last two verbs in verse 5 make an interesting couplet.

In verse 6 the psalmist takes his eyes off the enemy and focuses on God. The familiar, "Blessed be the LORD," begins this praise section. Again, note that it is written from the perspective of a prayer already answered. Or it may be understood that he blessed God in the light of former prayers and in anticipation that this one, too, would shortly get a response.

Verse 7 is rich with praise and joy. In military terms the psalmist asserts: "The LORD is my strength and my shield." He testifies that he trusts with his heart, not just with his lips. But it is with his lips that he will sing his song of praise.

The beneficiaries of God's blessing, as described in verse 8, may be plural or singular. The text can read either "The Lord is his strength" or "The Lord is their strength." Perhaps David refers to himself in verse 8b, for he, as a king of Israel, is one of God's anointed. His prayer definitely is not selfish as he concludes this psalm. God's people and His inheritance are one and the same thing.

At the very end of the psalm, David moves to a pastoral figure of speech as lovely as those in the Twenty-third Psalm. Among the tasks a shepherd has is to carry the lambs. We are God's lambs, and He will carry us forever.

PSALM 29

In this psalm God is exquisitely portrayed through the storm in verses 3-10. This hymn begins with two verses enjoining worshipers to ascribe glory to God. It ends with a benediction for God's people.

The opening lines illustrate a variety of staircase parallelisms (ABC, ABD, ABE). The first two important words (*give, Lord*) in each of the first three lines are the same. The third element changes. In the first line, the third element is *sons of the mighty*. Then it is *glory and strength*. In the third line it is *the glory of His name*.

For the difficult term in verse 1 (cf. Gen 6:2), the King James Version has "O ye mighty" and the Revised Standard

Version renders "O heavenly beings." Are these angels? Are they heathen deities? Are they extra strong, mighty men? Are they the spiritual sons of God, the true worshipers, the devout Yahwists? The last seems best. Furthermore, the parallel in the benediction (v. 11) is *His people*.

The last part of the fourth stich (v. 2b) has given rise to at least three interpretations. When rendered *holy array* (ASV, RSV) it seems that the worshiper or, at least, the officiating priest must be dressed in a certain way. The translation *in the beauty of holiness* (KJV) suggests the splendor of a place of worship. A third interpretation places the focus on the beauty of the Lord Himself, "at the manifestation of His holiness" (author's trans.). He, the holy One, is arrayed.

The middle section, the hymn itself, has many fascinating features. The name of the Lord appears in almost every stich—a total of eighteen times in the entire psalm. The expression "the voice of the LORD" occurs seven times. Another feature is the poetic balance within the entire section. *Waters* and *flood* appear in verses 3a and 10a, respectively. The *thunder* of 3b corresponds to the *lightning* of verse 7. The *power of His voice* in verse 4 corresponds to its shaking the desert in verse 8. The calf and the calving of verses 6 and 9a correspond.

Obviously the psalmist is illustrating the glory of God from natural phenomena. In this section there are no people—just God and nature. His power is most evident in the middle of a raging storm. It is impossible to explain all these figures from a scientific viewpoint. But witness the glory of God in the violence of nature as well as in the ancient poet's description. The worshiper hears God's whisper in the rain and His shout in the thunder. It is a powerful and majestic voice. Even the cedars of Lebanon, among the strongest trees in the world, break in the wind and are splintered by lightning bolts. The cedars of Lebanon prompt the psalmist to think of the mountains of Lebanon and of Sirion, as Mount Hermon was called (Deu 3:9).

Verse 6 should be scanned so that one geographical reference occurs in each of the two stichs (cf. RSV, NEB, JB, etc.). So not only the trees on the mountains sway, but the mountains themselves appear to shudder at God's voice. Anyone who has ever been caught on a mountain during a storm can testify to the awesomeness of the experience.

Lightning is described in verse 7 as God showering sparks as He strikes flinty stone with a metal tool. The uninhabited areas near Kadesh (probably the Kadesh to the north of Palestine), likewise tremble (v. 8).

Some translators alter the Hebrew slightly to make the *deer* (*hinds,* KJV) into *oaks* in verse 9a (RSV, JB). Such a change fits the immediate parallel with 9b much better, but it destroys the parallel with the *calf* and *young wild ox* (v. 6). (The KJV's *unicorn,* a fabled creature, is not an accurate translation of the Hebrew.)

Verse 10 provides a transition to the benediction. *Flood,* the translation of a Hebrew word found only in Genesis 6-11 and here, may refer to God's agent of punishment during the time of Noah. In fact, the entire hymn may be a veiled allusion to His wrath on His enemies, who are depicted here as stately trees and lofty mountains. Most of the figures used in the poem are also found in Ugaritic poems sung to Baal.

The benediction (v. 11) can be translated as a simple future or a jussive: "The Lord will give . . ." or "May the Lord give. . . ." Whereas His people had ascribed strength to Him (v. 1), He now gives strength to them. He will bless His people with *shalom*—physical, emotional, mental, financial, spiritual, and social well-being. It means peace with God, peace with others, and peace with oneself.

73

PSALM 30

Psalm 30 is a song of thanksgiving for deliverance from death. Some of the verses suggest it was a narrow escape from enemies (e.g., v. 1b) while others point to some physical illness (e.g., v. 2). Most of the content focuses on the actual plight of the poet rather than on the delivering power of God. It is very personal and therefore very easily applicable.

The title to this psalm seems wholly inappropriate. Some have suggested that the psalm titles, or parts of them, belong at the end of the psalms and not at the beginning. That suggestion is welcome in this case, for at least the temple was mentioned in Psalm 29 (v. 9). If the dedication of the house refers to the events of 1 Kings 8, where Solomon dedicated the temple he built, then there is a problem with the Davidic authorship of this psalm.

The psalm does not quickly betray its outline. Verse 1 is an introduction, while verses (11-12) are the conclusion. The body has several major themes: verses 2-3 constitute a testimony of salvation; verses 4-5 are instructions to others; verses 6-10 are a recitation of the actual lament uttered during the crisis.

David was disliked by many. From the time he killed Goliath until his own death, jealous men on all sides, and even within his own household, tried to kill him. Any one of those narrow escapes might be the basis for this song.

This poet, as all poets, must be granted some license to exaggerate. *Sheol* is the place of the dead. No mortal man returns from that place. It may seem that death is all around, but, in fact, the psalmist is kept alive, as the latter part of verse 3 indicates.

Verse 4 contains two noteworthy expressions. *Saints* is from the Hebrew word *hesed*. It means faithful, covenant

74

love. Usually God possesses *hesed,* not men. Nevertheless, the Hebrew describes the beneficiaries of *hesed* with the same word. The Hasidim, a very orthodox Jewish sect, derive their name from the same word. The other noteworthy expression is *memorial* or *remembrance.* A literal translation might be *the memory of His holiness.* It means: "We shall give thanks every time we remember how holy our God is." The pleasure of that memory is elaborated in verse 5.

Among the lovely twists and turns of this poet's pen are the heart-warming phrases of verse 5. There is no better way to say it than as he said it. Here is a literal translation:

> For a moment is His anger.
> For a lifetime is His favor.
> For an evening weeping lasts,
> But in the morning, singing.

If verse 6 sounds like boasting, it is only boasting in God. The psalm is written by a man who lived a God-centered life. When he was in danger, God delivered him; when he was ill, God healed him. Now, God has allowed him to fall into trouble, and the psalmist seeks His help. The opening of the lament evidences a belief that God will not let him fall. He is sure of his deliverance, but this is a discipline of faith and patience.

In verse 9 the sufferer uses an old tool to move God to respond. It is a variety of the "for-Your-name's-sake" argument. Like an oriental bargainer, he makes God weigh the cost against the benefit, the price against the worth.

Apparently the device worked, for the psalmist testifies that God turned his mourning into dancing. He removed his funeral garb and dressed him with joy—both interesting metaphors. For this and other benefits he sings praise and gives thanks forever. The highly personal psalm ends, as it began, jubilantly.

Psalm 31 is a blend of lament, prayer, testimony, and admonition, but none of these themes is dominant. Verses 1-18
are mostly prayer and lament. Verses 19-24 are mostly
testimony and admonition. As with the preceding psalm, the
troubles seem to be both illness and enemies. The figures
used are vivid and colorful.

Despite confessions of trust sprinkled throughout the first
part of the psalm, the content is basically a complaint. The
opening line is a statement of faith, but then the psalmist
launches into petition. The ancient saint feared the shame
of defeat. Any kind of loss not only humiliated him but his
family, his tribe, the cause he struggled for, and his God.
The psalmists founded many of their arguments on the basis
that God might be shamed. Spelled out more fully, the last
stich of verse 1 argues: Lord, if You are righteous You will
deliver me. If deliverance doesn't come, You will be accused
of unrighteousness.

The same logic shows up again in verse 5. These words
used both by Christ and by Stephen (Lk 23:46; Ac 7:59)
could be connected with what follows by the word *since*.
We should entertain no hesitancy in committing ourselves to
God, who has committed Himself to redeem us.

Other verses containing testimony of faith are 6-8, 14, and
15. Other verses with petitions in them are 2, 3, and 15-17.
Verse 3 in particular illustrates the way the psalmist "pres-
sures" God. He reminds God that His reputation is at stake.

The enemy is amply described in the other parts of the
first eighteen verses. In the prayers for deliverance from them
and in the imprecations against them, we have a vivid picture. According to verse 4, they secretly spread a net for the
righteous. According to verse 6, they are the guardians of
vain lies.

Beginning with verse 9, either the enemy is the "sickness" or David describes the physical effects of being hated. Diagnosis of a disease he may have had is impossible from these sketchy poetic phrases. His eye *wasted*. His strength *failed*. His bones *wasted*. Because of the phrase tucked away in verse 10, "because of my iniquity," the great enemy may have been within—his own sinful proclivity. Perhaps this psalm should be read with Psalm 51, the one connected with the king's confession of sin with Bathsheba. Notice verses 11 and 12, especially, in light of this suggestion.

Another suggestion for the life situation of this psalm is David's feigned insanity recorded in 1 Samuel 21:13. Verse 12a may allude to that incident.

The end of verse 13 marks a minor turning point in the psalm. In verse 14 the frustration and pessimism immediately give way to exuberant, positive faith. The little words *but God* make all the difference in the world. Though the enemies surround, though mortal life is in the balance, though personal sins weigh heavily, though the dawn appears never to come, yet we trust. And we say with David, "Thou art my God. My times are in thy hands."

Verses 15-18 contain a series of imperatives calling for God's blessing on the suppliant and for His curses on the wicked.

Blessing begins in verse 9. That verse and the following are addressed to God. Verse 21 speaks of God in the third person. These triumphs are uttered from the perspective of answered prayer. The "trouble and trust" sequence is once more demonstrated. Whether these ancient writers had an about face as they voiced their complaints to God, or whether they recorded their spiritual pilgrimages from the perspective time provided, is unknown. The important thing is that we bear in mind, even in times of deepest despair, that God is good.

The last two verses are injunctions to believers. The first command is to love God. Remember that these words were written by a man acquainted with the Ten Commandments. Seeing the first and greatest commandment in this context should be no surprise. The second and third admonitions are "be strong" and "take courage." These are similar to the orders given to Joshua (1:6, 7, 9). If we hope in the Lord as we say we do, then we should be strong and courageous of heart. In the past, God has mercifully preserved the faithful. He has adequately and abundantly punished the proud.

PSALM 32

Several verses of Psalm 32 have a familiar ring to them. Some are quoted in the New Testament. Others simply have endeared themselves to God's people over the years.

In this psalm, David draws special attention to the blessedness of sins forgiven and of a wholesome trust in the never-failing God. He had experienced sin and he had experienced forgiveness and therefore was qualified to write this poem.

Verses 1-2 introduce the subjects of sin and forgiveness. The word *blessed* is the same as the one that begins the first psalm. It could be translated "happy." Verse 1 is a close parallelism while verse 2 is freer poetry.

When the apostle Paul discussed imputation of sin in Romans 4 he alluded to these two verses (Ro 4:7-8). The doctrine of imputation is a great and precious one. Unfortunately, it is often misunderstood. Verse 2 does not say that certain men may sin and yet be innocent. It does not teach that some men have not sinned. Rather, the doctrine is that when God forgives sin it is reckoned to us no more. The New Testament elaborates on this by making clear that our sin is imputed to Christ and His righteousness is imputed to us (Ro 4:24, 25; 5:19, etc.). Verse 2 cannot be understood apart from verse 1. If one should have a guile-free spirit it is because God has forgiven his transgressions and covered his sin. True bliss, genuine happiness, comes from the assurance that God has forgiven sin. However incomplete was David's understanding of God's plan of salvation through Christ, he knew this one basic truth—God must forgive his sin.

Verses 3-7 describe the spiritual pilgrimage from the agony of unconfessed sin to the joy of certain deliverances. First, the psalmist relates the physical torment he endured. The price of keeping silent was wasting bones, day-long groaning, and dehydration. David understood what modern psychology has only recently discovered—many ills are caused by unconfessed sin. Many diseases are purely psychosomatic. Spiritual maladjustment often provokes physical ailment.

The turning point and apex of the psalm are verse 5. The sinner acknowledged his sin. He stopped trying to hide his iniquity. He confessed his transgressions. Then he arrived at that blessed state which the opening verses described—the state of forgiven sin.

Verse 6 is a homily on the preceding experience. Any believer can be godly. Any believer can pray. Any kind of trouble can threaten him, but never should it harm him. God is the hiding place for the saint. He will preserve him and circle him with song.

Another *selah* closes this major section as others did the minor breaks at verses 4 and 5.

The subject of verse 8 is uncertain. This may be one of the "songs of deliverance" that God gives, or it may be the advice of the experienced psalmist to his fellowman. The former is the usual interpretation of this dearly-loved promise. The picture is one of a father or a teacher closely watching every move of the son or the student. Unbelievers are unhappy at the thought that God sees everything they do, but this same fact is a source of comfort and joy to the child of God.

A most homey and rural illustration follows in verse 9. Everyone knows how much discipline dumb animals need. The exhortation is not to be like them. The interpretation of the American Standard Version is preferable for the end of verse 9. As draft animals need trappings to bring them into line so, too, God's children need discipline to keep them in line.

Verse 10 begins the conclusion to the psalm. As the poem started in general terms, so in general terms it ends. The wicked will reap sorrow, but believers inherit God's never-failing, covenant love.

The congregation and the reader are encouraged to gladness and joy in the concluding verse. Three imperative verbs outline this exhortation: *be glad, rejoice,* and *shout for joy.* The basis for such jubilation should be our standing in Christ. We are the happy ones whose transgressions are forgiven and whose sins are covered.

PSALM 33

Psalm 33 is a hymn. It has no title indicating the author, the occasion, or the purpose. After three verses of introduction enjoining worshipers to praise God, comes the body of the psalm (vv. 4-19), describing God's character and achievements. The last three verses constitute the pledge, promise, and prayer of the worshipers.

Five imperatives are in the opening three verses. Verse

80

1b is not an imperative but a novel twist on words to urge people to praise. It is a lovely thing for the upright to praise the Lord.

Several themes appear in the body of the psalm. Verses 4-5 speak of the faithfulness of God. Verses 6-9 focus on the creation by divine fiat. Verses 10-12 concern God's role in international politics. Verses 13-15 have to do with God's omniscience. And verses 16-19 teach the futility of trusting in human means and methods and the surety of God's deliverance.

Christians constantly need to be reminded of God's sovereignty. As verse 4 teaches, all God's doings are right and faithful. God is not prompted by selfishness or greed. He sets the standard of righteousness. All truth, all right, all justice are measured against His norm. Entire studies could be made on each of the key words in verses 4 and 5: *right, faithfulness, righteousness, justice,* and *lovingkindness.*

Perhaps even better than Genesis 1, the section beginning with verse 6 and ending with verse 9 teaches that God created the world out of nothing simply by speaking. The term *Word* suggests the second person of the Trinity (Jn 1:1-3). The word *breath* in verse 6b might even allude to the third person of the Trinity since *breath, wind,* and *spirit* are the same word in Hebrew. The term occurs in Genesis 1:2.

Verse 7 is a simile. Following the Greek and Latin versions, some modern translations read *wineskin* instead of *heap.* Implicit in verses 6-9 is the command of verse 8.

From the subject of the world in general, the hymn moves to the nations and peoples who occupy them (vv. 10-12). Whereas human plots and programs are often vetoed by God, His counsels and thoughts endure forever. No one can frustrate divine plans. Notice the perfect parallels in these two verses and how the words *counsel* and *thoughts* tie them together. Unlike other nations, whose schemes fail, the God-fearing nation will enjoy only success. With the Lord as their King, subjecting themselves to His gracious rule, they will be blessed indeed.

As noted above, verses 13-15 deal with God's all-seeing ability. Not only does He see every move men make and hear every word they say, but God also has made all men and can discern even their motives and attitudes.

The weak arm of the flesh and the strong arm of the Lord are the subjects of the following four verses. These verses also teach God's sovereignty. It is not the size of the army that wins the battle. It is God. It is not the strong man's strength that saves him. It is God. If God does not deign to deliver, then to rely on a horse is vain. Psalm 127:1 is a commentary on these thoughts:

> Except the Lord build the house,
>   they labor in vain that build it:
> Except the Lord keep the city,
>   the watchman wakes in vain.

Sure deliverance comes only to those who fear God and hope in His covenant faithfulness, which evidences itself in constant lovingkindness. God can also save their souls. Horses, strength, and armies cannot. When God's people face starvation, physical or spiritual, God will provide.

The concluding three verses express the self-dedication of the worshipers. They correspond to the hymns of commitment that close many modern church services. Each verse has two parts, an effect and a cause. The worshipers say, "Our soul has hoped in the Lord," the reason being that He is their help and shield. They promise that their hearts shall rejoice, the reason being that they have trusted in His holy name. They pray for God's loving-kindness on themselves, the reason being that they have hoped in Him.

82

O magnify the LORD with me
  and let us exalt his name together (v. 3).
The angel of the LORD encamps round about them that fear him,
  and delivers them (v. 7).
O taste and see that the LORD is good (v. 8a).'

These and other verses in Psalm 34 have endeared themselves to God's people over the centuries. This psalm is a
personal song of thanksgiving, on the one hand, and a wisdom psalm on the other. In it David recounts his deliverance
and adjures others likewise to trust in God.

The title alludes either to 1 Samuel 21:10-15, where
David feigned madness before King Achish of Gath, or to
some unrecorded similar incident. Achish may also have
been named Abimelech. There is nothing in the text of the
psalm which helps to pinpoint the situation.

Psalm 34 is another acrostic. Although there are the expected twenty-two verses corresponding to the twenty-two
letters of the Hebrew alphabet, the letter *vav* is missing and
verse 22 is beyond the end of the alphabet. The psalmist apparently labored to fit his material to this scheme, for there
is a certain lack of logic to the content. The subject matter
and the addresses change several times in the course of the
twenty-two verses.

Opening the psalm are two verses of personal praise. In
rather general terms, David sets the tone of the hymn.

Verse 3 is the first verse of exhortation. These words,
which frequently have been set to music, urge the listeners
to join the psalmist in exalting God's name.

The personal testimony begins in verse 4 with the statement that God has answered and delivered. Except for
verses 11 and 13, the balance of the testimony is in the third

person. It is clear, however, that David includes himself among those who fear God (v. 7) and are righteous (v. 15).

The *they* of verse 5 is without direct antecedent, but it must refer to the meek of verse 2 or the god-fearers of verse 7. Countenance reveals whether or not a life is lived by faith. Believers should be radiant. Confused looks and anxious faces belong to unbelievers. God's angel is our safety. From Hagar in Genesis 16:7 to the last book of the Old Testament, the angel of the Lord ministered to God's people.

Verses 8-9 continue the admonition to commitment. An invitation that is still valid is, "Taste and see that the Lord is good." A man cannot know blessedness until he takes refuge in God. A man cannot know freedom from want until he fears God. Verse 10 ends this brief section with a tidbit of wisdom akin to the Proverbs: Lions may get hungry but God's people will never lack.

Almost as if David were beginning a new psalm, verse 11 reinvites listeners to live God-fearing lives. This is followed by a series of proverb-like instructions. All men fit into the category of verse 12—all men want to be happy and live long. The how-to-do-it comes in verses 13 and 14. The timeless maxim of guarding the tongue appears here 1,000 years before Christ. What we say probably provokes more anguish than any single thing in our lives. The tongue is capable of the grossest iniquity. With it we can curse men or bless God.

The second set of instructions (v. 14) is general but universally applicable. "Seek good and not evil" was reiterated by the prophets (Is 1:16-17; Amos 5:14-15). "Seek peace" is echoed by the apostles (Ro 14:19; Heb 12:14). Elsewhere the manifold meaning of *shalom* (peace) is found (cf. Ps 29:11). The command is to do all you can to have everything right within yourself and with you, your neighbor, and God.

Verses 15-16 go together. The eyes and ears of the Lord are ready to see, hear, and help the good. But His face—meaning His favor—is against the wicked. The lot of evildoers is to have their remembrance removed from the earth. Would that only good men were remembered and the wicked forgotten. The word *remembrance* also has the meaning of *posterity*.

The testimony of praise resumes in verse 17. David probably is making veiled references to himself in these verses. The truth remains, however, that God loves and saves the humble from all sorts of grievous troubles. In specific terms, God does not let even a bone be broken. Some read into this verse an allusion to the fact that Jesus died without any bones broken. Such an interpretation is forcing a Messianic reference into the text.

The psalm concludes with two verses that form a pair much as verses 15-16 do. First the psalmist predicts the fate of the wicked and then testifies to the deliverance of the servants of God. The verdict will be "innocent" for those whose refuge is in God. Whereas the wicked condemn the righteous (v. 21), God vindicates them (v. 22).

PSALM 35

Psalm 35 is an imprecatory psalm. In it David calls down numerous curses on his enemies. Then he looks forward to rejoicing when God will punish them for all their wrong. The first complaint section runs from verse 1 to verse 8. Then follow two verses promising praise. Verses 11-17 are a mixture of accusation and self-justification. Verse 18 corresponds to verses 9-10 as a vow to give thanks. The imprecations continue in verses 19-26. The psalm concludes with yet more pleas for and pledges of praise.

In the light of the teaching of our Lord Jesus Christ, many find it hard to understand such cursing on the enemy as occurs in this and other psalms. How could God inspire a man to pen such venom? How can a psalm like this serve as a stimulus to piety? Should a Christian use such imprecations against others? Such questions are not easily answered.

Perhaps one explanation is found in the nature of the hatred mentioned here. It is a holy hatred. David viewed these enemies not so much as his own personal foes, but as adversaries of God and of God's nation, and of God's plan. The king so identified himself with the kingdom of God on earth that any opposition to it was opposition to God. The enemies were not under God's covenant. They were not believers. They were not concerned with the progress of Israel. Therefore, they must be cursed.

Secondly, a difference between the Old and New Testaments admittedly does exist: missionary obligations were nonexistent or unclearly understood by our Old Testament forebears. In their minds, God had only one chosen people and they were the citizens of Israel. Only with the coming of Christ did it become unquestionably obvious that God has chosen people from all nations, that His Kingdom is not of this world, and that He loves all men.

A third answer is in the cold facts themselves. Men were trying to kill David. It is the normal reaction of regenerate and unregenerate men alike to resist death and to love life. These wicked men were liars, cheaters, defrauders, murderers, and false accusers. David could not have been expected to condone and bless their evil.

A fourth answer or application is to recognize that the enemies of the Gospel are either willing agents or unconscious tools of the devil. These psalms can be used in our spiritual warfare described in Ephesians 6:11-18 to fight the wicked one who is the mastermind behind the human persecutors.

In the first eight verses are seven verbs in the imperative and seven in the jussive form ("let them . . ."). Most of them are curses on the enemy; a few are prayers for the protagonist himself.

The Jerusalem Bible has a very clipped but accurate rendering of the first verse. The translation is very close to the Hebrew.

> Accuse my accusers, Yahweh,
> attack my attackers.

The terminology of the first four verses is military: "take hold of shield and buckler . . . draw out the spear." From these the poet turns to expressions which might be found in the everyday life of hunting and agriculture: "chaff . . . a dark and slippery way . . . their net," etc. Note the presence of the angel of the Lord in verses 5-6. In the former verse he drives them like chaff and in the latter he chases them down a muddy path at night. Verses 7-8 are linked in a manner typical of the psalms. Whereas the enemy hid a net and dug a pit to trap the righteous, the prayer is that God would use these same devices to trap the wicked.

The first promises to praise are in verses 9-10. As though he anticipated the answer to his prayers, David pledges his praise to God for his deliverance. The expression "all the bones" means simply "with the entire being" (cf. Ps 34:20).

The section from verses 1-17 is a mixture. Verses 11-12 are complaints against the activity of the ungodly. The scene is in a court of law and the complaint is against lying witnesses who bring trumped-up charges against the psalmist.

Verses 13-14 are David's self-justification. Perhaps Christians ought to focus on these verses rather than on the imprecations. Despite all the evident hatred David had for his enemies, there is no reason to doubt the boasts of verses 13f. He declares that he sympathized when they mourned and felt afflicted himself when they grieved. But most of all he withdrew his prayer against them, at least temporarily. When his enemies suffered, then he treated them as brothers.

Such a gracious spirit does not last long, for complaints about the enemies' antagonistic activities resume in verse 15. They mocked. They gnashed. They rejoiced at David's calamity. A plea for God to act closes this section. It is as if the cases have been laid before the judge and now the accused, speaking on his own behalf, begs for a favorable and just decision from the bench.

Again, in verse 18, he promises to thank and praise God when it is all over. This verse corresponds to 9f. and 28.

The imprecations of verses 19 and 25f. introduce and conclude, respectively, the complaints and pleas of verses 20-24. In particular, verses 20-21 describe the conspiracy the enemy concocted against the righteous. With winks and chuckles they enjoyed their crafty prosperity. So David pleads with God to wake up, take notice, and do something to vindicate him. Four curses in the jussive form constitute verses 25-26 and close the imprecatory parts of this psalm.

The same verb form continues in verse 27 as David prays that the righteous be given cause to rejoice. That cause is a verdict of innocence for the good and a sentence of guilty for the wicked.

The last promise to praise comes as a benediction and conclusion to the entire psalm. As a result of a favorable and just decision, the psalmist vows that his tongue shall talk of God's righteousness and praise all day long.

PSALM 36

Psalm 36 partakes of the characteristics of the imprecatory psalms but only in a minor way. A better balance prevails between complaints because of the wickedness of sinful men and praise for the loving-kindness of God.

The opening four verses describe the wicked. The closing two verses are prayer and prediction of deliverance. The middle section, verses 5-10 focuses on God's benign attributes.

Some key words expand this rudimentary, chiastic structure. The words "wicked" and "iniquity" appear in verses 1-4 and 11-12. "Lovingkindness" and "righteousness" link verses 5-6 to verse 10.

Modern comparative Semitic language study has discovered that the difficult *my heart* in verse 1 can be read "his heart." This does not alter the Hebrew text and at the same time provides an easier reading. The verb in verse 1 (*saith*) is the usual word for divine utterances and generally is found when the prophets introduce God's speeches. Here the point must be that wicked men listen to their hearts rather than to God. So they come up with the blasphemous attitude described in verse 1b and following (cf. Ro 3:18).

Through verse 4 the servant of the Lord delineates the wicked man's thought pattern. He begins with a certain godlessness. Then pride pervades his thinking. Soon he is convinced that his sin will not be discovered or punished. He proceeds to voice his plots, which are neither wise nor good. Having worked out the iniquity while lying in bed, he then executes his wicked chicanery.

A major break in the subject matter comes with verse 5. Now the mercy, faithfulness, righteousness, and justice of God are in view. These attributes, limitless in their scope, sustain the universe. God preserves man and beast, but particularly man. He may enjoy the shade from His wings. He may feast on the abundance of His house. He may imbibe the water from the river of His pleasures.

God is the source of all life and light. A preferable translation makes verse 9b into a prayer: "In thy light let us see light." This simple half verse could be expanded in several directions. The first and most obvious interpretation is that we are blind apart from the divine illumination of the Holy Spirit. Or the phrase may be a prayer to see things from God's perspective in the light of eternity. A third line of interpretation is that the study of God's Word under godly instructors affords an appetite and an ability to understand even more truth. Such an interpretation is borne out by verse 10. David prays that God's loving-kindness and righteousness might endure and multiply.

The prayer portion of this psalm may begin in the middle of verse 9 or only at verse 10. Either way verses 10-11 form a couplet. Verse 10 is positive. Verse 11 is negative. In the former, David begs for continued mercy. In the latter he pleads deliverance from evil of two sorts. He needs to be saved from the sin of pride (cf. v. 12), and he needs to be rescued from the wicked hands of godless men.

The last verse elaborates on the fate of those iniquitous men. They are fallen, thrown down, and made unable to rise. Judgment always has two sides. The righteous are exonerated and delivered while the wicked are convicted and punished. Christians have been saved from hell and for heaven. Sinners forfeit heaven and inherit hell.

PSALM 37

The English reader does not appreciate the alphabetic outline of Psalm 37 but it is nevertheless there. The psalmist sought to begin every other verse with each successive letter of the alphabet. Verse 1 begins with the first letter of the Hebrew alphabet, verse 3 with the second, verse 5 with the third, and so forth.

Besides being alphabetic, the psalm is also an elaborate chiasmus. Here is that outline:

1-8	A	The righteous are exhorted to ignore the wicked and trust God.
9	B	Wait and inherit the land.
10-15	C	The righteous inherit but the Lord destroys the plotting wicked.
16	D	The poor are blessed though poor.
17	E	The Lord upholds the righteous.
18a	F	The Lord guides the righteous.
18b	G	The righteous inherit.
19	H	The righteous get.
20a	I	The wicked perish.
20b	J	The wicked are like a sacrifice.
20c	J'	The wicked are like a sacrifice.
21a	I'	The wicked give not.
21b	H'	The righteous give.
22	G'	The blessed inherit.
23	F'	The Lord guides the righteous.
24	E'	The Lord upholds.
25-26	D'	The blessed may be poor but not forsaken.
27-33	C'	The Lord loves the righteous who will live and inherit, but the plotting wicked will die.
34	B'	Wait and inherit the land.
35-40	A'	God destroys the wicked but saves the righteous.

Such devices have nothing to do with the meaning of the psalm, but to learn of such fascinating details can draw from us a greater interest in and appreciation for the literary excellence of God's holy Word.

A simpler outline based on broad themes might be this:

    A. Counsel for the meek (1-11)
    B. Warning for the wicked (12-20)
    C. Reward for the righteous (21-31)
    D. Contrasts of retributions (32-40)

The basic message of the psalm is the safety and blessing of those who trust in God and the insecurity of the ungodly. Many of the verses are proverb-like, and for this reason we might classify it as a wisdom psalm. Proverbs 24:19 is almost exactly like verse 1:

> Fret not yourself because of evildoers,
>   and be not envious of the wicked.

The sixteenth verse is like Proverbs 15:16 and 16:8:

> Better is a little with righteousness
>   than great revenues with injustice.

In addition, there are several well-known proverbs found only here. One of them is verse 21. It reads:

> The wicked borrows and pays not again,
>   but the righteous deals graciously and gives.

Verse 25 is used in the Jewish prayer after meals:

> I have been young, and now am old;
>   Yet have I not seen the righteous forsaken
>   Nor his seed begging bread.

The imagery of verse 35 is also well known:

> I have seen the wicked in great power,
>   And spreading himself like a green tree.

The first seven verses of the psalm are hortatory, and with these we will deal in some detail. A numbering of the imperatives reveals that there are four *do not*s and eight *do*s. Verses 1, 7, and 8 instruct us to "fret not." Basically the meaning of the word is "to anger yourself." A colloquial translation would be, "Don't fume" or "Don't get burned up." Although there may be a place for righteous indignation, Christians by and large ought to refrain from anger. "Fret not." In view of eternity, in view of the fact that we are called to please God and not men, in view of the uselessness of getting angry, in view of the coming judgment, and in view of our God who will adjudicate all injustices, we ought not to fret because of evildoers.

The second negative imperative is like the above: "Be not envious." Although jealousy can be commendable in cases such as that of Phinehas (Num 25:11-13, NASB), generally it is not a wholesome characteristic. Rachel, Joseph's brothers, and Absalom are examples of the bad kind of jealousy or envy. For the reasons noted above, envy is warned against.

The other two warnings are in verse 8: "Cease from anger, and forsake wrath." These are obviously parallel to the above two warnings, except that the words are prohibitions in themselves and do not need the particle *not* to make them negative.

The eight *do*s are the heart of the psalm and are found in the most popular verses. Verses 3-5 enjoin us to trust the Lord. Coupled with our spiritual, or soul, reaction is the practical injunction, "do good." In terms of God's economy, good deeds done prior to faith are of no avail. On the other hand, "faith without works is dead" (Ja 2:20).

The latter half of verse 3 also has two imperatives, though they are not so rendered in the Authorized Version. Listen to the translation from the 1901 American Standard Version:

> Trust in Jehovah and do good;
> Dwell in the land, and feed on his faithfulness.

The last word might also be rendered *truth*. With the elimination of the added word *his* it would read: "Feed on truth."

Verse 4 has both a command and a blessed promise. The linking of these two is significant. When we delight in the Lord, we want what He wants. Then what we ask will be in His will. The desires of our heart will be the desires of His heart.

As noted above, verse 5 begins with the third letter of the Hebrew alphabet. The inspired author chose the word which has the basic meaning of "roll." Hence the imperative "commit" could be translated "roll." This idea is reflected in 1 Peter 5:7: "Casting all your care upon Him; for He cares for you." A popular chorus goes "Every burden of my heart rolled away." Proverbs 16:3 has the same verb and thought.

The last two commands of this section are in verse 7 and are parallel. "Rest in the Lord, and wait patiently for him." *Wait patiently* really means "to writhe," or "to wrestle in conflict," hence to make fervent supplication to God. So here is a paradox: rest, but wrestle. Sometimes this is the hardest command of all to obey. Yet this is just what some of God's people need most. This is advice for the sick, the fretful, the anxious, and the faithless.

The remainder of the psalm is to encourage the saints of God, to show them the end of the wicked and the blessed destiny of the righteous. That destiny is found, among other places, in the last verse:

> And the LORD shall help them,
> and deliver them:

He shall deliver them from the wicked,
   and save them,
Because they trust in him.

PSALM 38

Psalm 38 is an individual lament. A reading of the opening verses leaves the impression that David was physically
sick. One might follow two lines of reasoning to explain
this and similar psalms. First, he may be writing with the
idea in mind that sickness is a punishment for sin. If he is
not, at least his associates thought that. The other line of
reasoning is that sin does have its psychosomatic effects. Ul-
cers, headaches, and hypertension are just three common
maladies provoked by worry, jealousy, or guilt.

Some of the verses are very much like Job's complaints.
The expression "arrows" of verse 2 is in Job 6:4. The reference to *bones* in verse 3 is similar to Job 33:19. The aloof-
ness of friends was the lot of this psalmist and Job alike.
Compare verse 11 with Job 19:13-19.

Psalm 38 is very human. The view of God is not too high.
David seems to understand sickness as God's wrath (vv. 1-
3). Many of God's children have felt the same way. As the
psalm develops, however, it becomes clear that God is only
indirectly responsible, for sin has its own reward. To suffer
for ignorance, foolishness, or disobedience does not require
a special act of God's retributive justice . Many daily illus-
trations prove that if we do not "follow the directions" we
suffer.

Verses 2-11 are written out of genuine agony. The sufferer creates a word picture with deftness and vividness.
God's arrows stick into him. God's hand squashes him (v.
2). The ancient understanding of anatomy as simply flesh

and bones appears in verse 3. Neither of these basic elements enjoy *shalom*—health. The pictures in verse 4 are of a man crushed by the weight of his sins. These figures are sustained in verses 6-7. Verse 5 describes open wounds while verse 7 may allude to some digestive disorder. Verses 8 and 10 show a man dizzy and bruised, with an overworked heart, tired muscles, and eyes without sparkle.

Only verse 9 is a breath of fresh air in this catalog of grief. David stops a moment to restate his confidence in God. On the other hand, he may be giving a gasp of despair. He says, in effect, God is my last and only hope. All the doctors, all the medicines, all the counsel, and all the advice have failed. As a last resort he hopes in God. How much like God's modern children! Instead of God being the first resort, He is often the last.

Sometimes the hardest pain to face is that of friendlessness. Verse 11 indicates that even his closest friends and relatives avoided him. Perhaps he had a contagious disease. Perhaps he was just a miserable person to be with and no one elected his company. Christians ought to examine their personalities, for often harbored in them are some horrribly offensive spiritual diseases.

From bodily disorders, David turns in verse 12 to the troubles caused by his enemies. Even though he had alluded to his own sin (vv. 3, 4) he still finds some comfort in cursing his enemies for his misfortunes. This may also be a spiritual illness on our part—blaming others for troubles that we bring on ourselves.

The psalmist asserts his innocence and nonretaliating spirit in verses 13-14, and gives the reason for such patience in verse 15. Verse 15 corresponds in its sentiment to verse 9. Verses 19-20 elaborate on the description of David's enemies.

If there is any development in the psalm, it begins in verses

16-17. There the psalmist sees the wisdom of affording the enemy no opportunity to rejoice over his plight. And again he sees the necessity to confess his sin and repent of his iniquity.

The psalm concludes with two verses of petition which answer to the opening plea of verse 1. "Forsake me not . . . be not far from me . . . make haste to help me." These wrap up the anguish and agony of a despairing saint. In the end, there is no salvation from Satan, from physical pain, from guilt-ridden lives, or from the hateful adversary other than in God and His never failing mercy.

PSALM 39

Jeduthun, who appears in the titles of Psalms 39, 62, and 77, was a musician mentioned in 1 Chronicles 16:41 and 25:1. The old questions rise again. Did Jeduthun write this about David? Was Jeduthun the chief musician? Is David the author of the words and someone else the composer of the tune to which they were sung? To none of these inquiries is there any definite answer.

Psalm 39 is both a wisdom psalm and a lament. It contains the personal complaint of a suffering saint (cf. v. 10). But it also has pithy bits of wisdom such as verse 5. Verses 5-6 in particular sound like the book of Ecclesiastes.

If *selah* does indicate some sort of a break, then its two occurrences in this psalm are somewhat appropriate. Verse 6 introduces a section focusing on the vanity of mankind in general and prompts a reaction from the psalmist. Verse 12 begins the concluding prayer.

Up to the middle of verse 3, the psalmist reflects on how quiet and patient he was about his troubles. Recognizing that the tongue produces innumerable problems, he decided at first against using it. But, as verse 3 indicates, all those pent-up feelings, all those harbored grudges, and all those unspoken emotions burned within him as he thought on them. The expression, "while I was musing, the fire burned," is often misunderstood. It is not a picture of a thinker in front of a fireplace but of a man with a fire on his insides. Jeremiah had a similar problem of God-sent heartburn (Jer 20:9).

Finally the silence breaks in verse 4. The words are a prayer to understand the frailty and brevity of life. The confession of verse 5 is pessimistic and discouraging, but also true. God can live without us. But without God, our lives are pure vanity.

The transition to verse 6 is very smooth as the psalmist enlarges on the subject introduced in verse 4: "Let me know how frail I am." The opening line of verse 6 more accurately translates as "man walks in a shadow." It may mean that man never sees things in full light and as they really are. Or it may mean, as some versions have it, that man's life is as brief and unimportant as a shadow. The things men fight for are usually fleeting. What a man gathers is soon dissipated, or dispersed to those who neither understand nor appreciate it.

All this pessimism prompts the confession and prayer of verses 7-8. While other men are hopeless, the psalmist affirms his hope in God. To the believer, life has direction, purpose, and fulfillment. Verse 8 has the only specific reference to sin. In the event that his troubled spirit is a result of sin, the psalmist prays for deliverance.

That plea is partly prompted by a fear of embarrassment. But the end of the psalm does not lead to the belief that in this poem the author was truly penitent.

More of the feelings of the protagonist surface in verse

98

9. Here he begins to blame God more directly for his troubles. The complaint against God grows more specific in
verse 10 as he lays the heavy charge on God for the strokes
and blows he has gotten. The complaint becomes even more
bitter in verse 11, as he charges God with making men be
consumed like moths as a price for their sin. A moth is a
very short-lived insect, and man's life is very short and vain
as well.

In spite of the overwhelming despair of the entire psalm,
verses 12-13 emit a vapor of hope. It is not enough, however, to turn the tide of pessimism. Acknowledging that he
is but a guest with God, he prays nevertheless for mercy
during his brief stay. No glimmer of hope of an afterlife
brightens the conclusion of this psalm. Rather, an embittered plea for respite from the avenging hand of God ends
this bleak poem.

PSALM 40

Psalm 40 can be divided into two parts. Verses 1-10 constitute a hymn of praise while verses 11-17 are a prayer for
deliverance. Psalm 70 is virtually identical to Psalm 40:13-
17.

Personal praise marks the first two and a half verses. The
description of the trouble David was in is very graphic. "He
brought me up also out of a horrible pit, out of the miry
clay." Jeremiah really had this happen to him (Jer 38:6).
David may be speaking in figurative terms just as we do when
we sing the gospel song based on those words. Some Bible
students make the entire psalm refer to Christ. On that basis,
these opening lines cannot be the believer's testimony, for

they are the Messiah's words. Such an approach is danger-
ous and open to abuse because it has no guidelines.

In the middle of verse 3, and continuing through verse 5,
the worshiper speaks more often in corporate terms. "Many
shall see . . . Blessed is the man (any man) . . . many are
your thoughts to us." In other words, in the middle of his
testimony he turns to preaching.

If this song immediately followed an illness such as those
alluded to in the preceding psalms, then it provides an interesting illustration of the benefits of sickness. Sometimes God
makes His children look up by putting them flat on their
backs. When things go well, it is easy to forget God and
our necessary dependence on Him. Only after God forced
him to take the time, did David realize just how many are
God's wonderful works and thoughts toward men. They are
innumerable. The gospel song "Count Your Many Blessings"
teaches the same truth in the line, ". . . name them one by
one, and it will surprise you what the Lord has done."

The author of the epistle to the Hebrews quotes most of
verses 6-8 (Heb 10:5-7) and applies the testimony to
Christ. Verse 6 repeats the truth Samuel told Saul (1 Sa
15:22). Isaiah echoed the same principle several hundred
years later (Is 1:11). In the New Testament the doctrine
is fully expounded. God does not want endless blood sacrifices. From the beginning, He has been interested in obedience. God knew that one day His Son would end all sacrifices in His own death.

The New Testament quotation of Hebrews 10:5-7 is from
the Greek translation of the Old Testament. That translation paraphrased the Hebrew "Ears thou hast digged for me"
into "A body thou hast prepared for me." No other suitable
explanation exists other than that the Septuagint scholars
thought a paraphrase rather than a strict translation would

best communicate the truth. The truth is that God must prepare the servant to understand. The unregenerate man has no capacity either to believe or behave rightly. A supernatural act of "fashioning the body" is required.

Verse 7 can be interpreted in two ways. One is that the *volume of the book* predicts the delight the Messiah will have in doing God's will. The other interpretation is that the "volume of the book" contains instructions to the saint to make God's will his delight. The Hebrew can be read either, "written to me" or "written of me." It is a toss-up as to which the ancient poet meant, since both renderings are grammatically correct, exegetically possible, and orthodox. The message remains: Christ did God's will and Christians are to be Christlike.

The first half of the psalm concludes with the testimony of verses 9-10. A mixture of positive and negative declarations mark these two verses. The psalmist did *not* refrain his lips. He did *not* hide God's righteousness. He did *not* conceal God's loving-kindness and truth. Rather, he *did* proclaim the good news. He *did* declare God's faithfulness and salvation. We might take a lesson from the nature of these statements. Not praising God is a sin. Perhaps among the sins of omission, one of the most frequently "committed" is thanklessness, or ingratitude. Worship does not end at noon on Sunday. Appreciativeness should be a way of life for the Christian. Those for whom God has done so much should ever be ready with a psalm, a hymn, or a spiritual song.

Prayer, confession, and imprecation mark verses 11-17. Confession is limited to verse 12 and the first line of verse 17. Not only have troubles from without disturbed David's fellowship with God, but sin from within weighed heavy on his spirit.

101

The imprecations are found in verses 14-15. The two verses divide into three synonymous parts. Three compound curses open each of the three parts and three phrases describing the enemies' acts close each part.

Balancing these prayers *against* the foe is the prayer *for* the fellow believers in verse 16. The remaining verses of this section (vv. 11, 13, 17) are David's prayers for his own deliverance. First he asks for mercy, loving-kindness, and truth (v. 11). Then more specifically he asks for help and deliverance (vv. 13, 17). The psalm ends on a note of urgency: "Don't wait, O my God!"

PSALM 41

A simple chiastic outline fits Psalm 41.

Praise to God (1-3)
    Prayer for mercy (4)
        Trouble from the enemy (5-9)
    Prayer for mercy (10)
        Triumph over the enemy (11-12)
Praise to God (13)

Obviously the larger blocks of verses deal with suffering from enemies. But the psalmist is also suffering from some illness or wound, if verse 3 is taken at all in its plain sense.

Inasmuch as verse 9b was quoted by Jesus in reference to Judas in John 13:18, this is also a Messianic psalm. Some not-so-conservative interpreters go a step further and make the entire psalm fit with the life of Christ. Such a course of interpretation requires that many of the details be ignored which more literally may have been applied to David.

Psalm 41 is the last psalm in the first book of the Psalter.

102

(Other divisions begin after Psalms 72, 89, and 106.) It begins with the same word that began Psalm 1: *blessed* or *happy*. A different Hebrew word, however, lies behind the *blessed* of verse 13.

The opening three verses describe the man who considers the poor and weak. What God will do for such a man makes up the content of those verses. By this means the psalmist gradually comes around to the subject of his own suffering. He hints at trouble in verse 1b; the idea takes shape in verses 2-3; finally in verse 4 he makes his point, "Heal me." The preceding generalities suddenly give way to specifics. All the introductory verses speak in the third person of a suffering man. Now in verse 4 it is "I . . . O LORD."

As in other psalms, the connection between sin, sickness, and enemies is not clear. Perhaps the poet's line of reasoning went this way: Sin removed God's blessing, which in turn resulted in a military defeat in which the hero was wounded. While recovering from those wounds he found time to think on God's faithfulness and justice, and on his own sin. Then he mixed his prayer for recovery and his confession with maledictions on the foe.

The central section, verses 5-9, contains some particularly caustic remarks. Verse 5 is especially cruel, for the enemy wished not only for the king's death but also for that of his entire family. *Name* can and should be understood to mean all the descendants who bear the progenitor's name.

Even the brief prayer for mercy in verse 10 has retaliation as its purpose. Notice the source of assurance in verse 11. David knows God is with him because God is against his enemy.

Verse 13 concludes both the forty-first psalm and the first book within the Psalter. It echoes both verse 1 of this psalm as well as parts of Psalm 1. The Hebrew word for *forever* occurs once in verse 12 and twice in verse 13. Not only does

103

David trust that God will give him everlasting life but also that God will get everlasting praise.

A double *amen* concludes the verse, the psalm, and the book (cf. Ps 72:19; 89:52; 106:48; 150:6). *Amen* is one of those few words that migrated intact from one language to another. Attempts to translate it—such as, "so be it," "it stands," or "I believe it"—lack the force of this one pure Hebrew word, *amen*.

PSALMS 42-43

Psalm 42 and 43 together constitute a single poem of three stanzas. A nearly identical chorus follows each stanza (42: 5, 11; 43:5). That Psalm 43 has no title is additional reason for putting the two together.

The title of Psalm 42 indicates that the psalm (or psalms) is for the chief musician, as many of the preceding ones have been. It also claims to be a *maschil* (a kind of psalm) of the sons of Korah. (Compare the titles in Psalms 44-49.) The Korahites were one of the families appointed to the ministry of music by David (cf. 1 Ch 6:31-37).

The first two stanzas, i.e., the whole of Psalm 42, are basically a personal lament. In the third stanza, Psalm 43, the psalmist turns to petitioning God. The psalms fit the "trouble and trust" category as well.

The opening verses are dear to many of God's children to this day. The picture is of a thirsty deer panting for a drink from a mountain brook. So the psalmist's soul, meaning the man himself, is anxious to meet God again. Until God satisfies his thirst, he must drink his own tears while plagued by adversaries who ask the taunting question, "Where is your God?"

The content of the recollections in verses 4-6 suggests an exilic background for this psalm. With fond memories and anguished yearning the psalmist brings to mind the delights of temple worship (v. 4), the thronging crowd of worshipers, the magnificent house of God, the enrapturing music, and the annual festivals.

We gain a different perspective on the church when its fellowship is denied us. That which can become so ordinary and even boring takes on different meaning when we are separated from it. After we had spent a week in an Islamic country on a Holy Land trip, a cathedral was the first stop in the next country. One pastor remarked on how refreshing it was to be in a church of any kind after being exiled, so to speak, in a culture with almost no Christian influence.

The chorus which closes the first stanza (v. 5) is a one-man dialogue. The poet addresses a question to his own soul and then proceeds to answer himself. In his mind he vascillates between pessimism and optimism, between despair and trust, between walking by sight and walking by faith, between looking at himself and his circumstances and looking at God and His will and ability.

Though the fifth verse ends on a somewhat positive note, verse 6 resumes the discouraged tone which prevails through these two psalms. This time, rather than remembering the temple worship, the exiled Judean brings to mind what may have been his homeland, the hills large and small along the Jordan valley. Especially in the flatlands of Mesopotamia—where the psalmist may have been exiled—would the recollection of mountains be particularly nostalgic.

Verse 7 is difficult to interpret. It is unlikely that the psalmist is drowning, which is the surface meaning. The latter half of the verse was quoted by Jonah, who could apply it to himself quite literally (Jon 2:3). Perhaps this is a highly figurative expression for being overwhelmed with

105

trouble. We use the expressions "snowed under" or "buried." Some scholars say that this verse, and perhaps the preceding one, is written from the vantage point of *sheol,* the abode of the dead. Even that would be hyperbole.

In the wavering course between despair and confidence in these psalms, verse 8 is again on the positive side. Not only are these lovely poetic lines, but they bespeak a wholesome and refreshing heart attitude. Elihu told of God's giving "songs in the night" (Job 35:10).

A mood of despair takes over in verses 9-10, which in turn introduce the chorus again. In verse 9 the psalmist, with conviction, blames God for absenting Himself in troublous times. Yet in other parts of the psalm the writer appears to be a man of little faith. He is unable to lift his eyes off the problem-plagued horizon and gain a clear perspective of God, whom he claims to trust.

The third stanza (Ps 43) begins with a plea for justice and an appeal for deliverance from deceitful and unjust men. The *ungodly nation* in verse 1 may be the Babylonians, who captured the psalmist and his people. Verse 2 is similar to Psalm 42:9 in that the latter halves are identical.

The appeal of verse 3 is addressed to God. The verse has been misapplied and used as an injunction to Christian witness and missions. The psalmist is in the dark and surrounded by deceitful men. Against this background he prays for some word from God to give him direction. He wishes to go to Jerusalem, God's holy hill, and to God's dwelling place there. Then he wants to go to the altar and join the orchestra that praises God. On this happy note the refrain begins for the third and last time:

> Why are you cast down, my soul?
>> Why are you disquieted within me?
> Hope in God;

106

For I shall yet praise him who saves my face,
My God.

PSALM 44

Psalm 44 can easily be divided into three parts. Verses
1-8 recollect former deliverances and victories. Verses 9-16
lament present trouble and defeat. Verses 17-26 are a mixture of protestations of trust and innocence with pleas for
help. Basically this psalm falls into the category of communal laments. It may have been written against the background of a specific military loss or in the light of the Babylonian exile itself. There is nothing else to indicate the occasion which prompted the poem.

The opening section (vv. 1-8) in and of itself is a fine
hymn of praise. As with the entire work, a militaristic and
mercantile vocabulary is present.

The psalmist recounts past deliverances which his fore-
fathers benefited from and enjoyed. His purpose is to build
up his historical argument. By this means psalmists and
prophets, as well as modern believers, have hoped to move
God to beneficent action. It is as if they were saying, "You
did it before, Lord; do it again."

Notice the parallels in the first verse: "We heard . . . they
told . . . In their days, the days of old." After this introduction, the psalmist begins to spell out the conquest of the
land in simple, graphic, but general terms. Verse 2 is a fine
illustration of antithetic parallelism. The first and the third
lines tell what God did to the other nations, while the second
and fourth lines tell what God did for His people. The first
two lines of verse 3 are negative, while the latter two lines

are positive. The first half tells how God's people did *not* fight and the second half tells how their God *did*.

Verse 4 is somewhat of a change of pace. It has the first occurrence of the word *my*. Only two other verses in the psalm are similarly personal, verses 6 and 15. Otherwise the work is strictly communal, that is, *we, us,* and *our* are the characteristic pronouns of the protagonist. Verse 4 is also a prayer which interrupts what is otherwise a praise section. Furthermore, there is a change of subject after verse 4.

In verse 5 the emphasis changes to trust. Inasmuch as the fathers were delivered from their enemies, so the psalmist hopes that his generation will enjoy similar victories. Verse 6 is like the first half of verse 3. Verse 7 probably recalls a more recent deliverance—one within living memory—which prompts the statement of faith in verse 8. The expression, "all the day long" occurs again in different contexts in verses 15 and 22.

If there ever was an appropriate place for *selah,* it is here at the end of verse 8, where it marks the major turning point of the psalm.

All the happy and inspiring reminiscences and pledges of trust in verses 1-8 give way to bitter complaint in verses 9 and following. God is charged with casting off and dishonoring His people. According to the psalmist, he has not accompanied the army, which was another cause for their defeat. That defeat is elaborated on in verses 10-11. It is the latter part of verse 11, together with verse 14, that particularly points to an exilic origin for this psalm.

The motif changes in verse 12 to that of a bad bargain in the market. God is accused of selling His people and losing money in the deal. The anguish is made more bitter by the rejoicing of blasphemous enemies (vv. 13-16).

The third section starts at verse 17 and continues to the end. Verses 17-18 are protestations of innocence and fidelity. The singers of this lament assert four times that they have not wavered in their allegiance to the one true God. In this respect this psalm is like the book of Job. For no reason apparent to the psalmist, God has dealt harshly with His own people. From time to time Christians are thrust into similar circumstances. Only an understanding of the kinds of suffering, and an unfeigned faith in the God who does only what is right, help in such trying times. Here, in outline form, are the different kinds of suffering mentioned in the Bible.

1. The natural results of foolishness or stupidity, illustrated in the parables and the proverbs by the poor investors (Mt 25:14-30; Pr 20:4).

2. God-allowed but Satan-sent, persecution of believers, illustrated by the troubles that beset the apostles in the book of Acts.

3. God-sent punishment for disobedience, illustrated by Korah and his rebellious company (Num 16) and by Ananias and Sapphira (Ac 5:1-11).

4. God-sent discipline to believers, illustrated by Moses not being allowed into the promised land. This kind, like the one above, has a didactic purpose.

5. God-ordered suffering sent to edify, but not caused by disobedience. It does not have correction as its aim but, rather, the glory of God and the building up of the saint. The man born blind (Jn 9:3), the parable of the vine (Jn 15:2), and Job illustrate this type.

The testimony of the sufferers in Psalm 44:17-19 then would classify this under the fifth type of suffering.

Verse 20 starts with *if* and is a kind of self-malediction. The believers invite God to search their hearts and check on secret sins (cf. Ps 19:12-13). Verse 22 contains more embittered complaint. Paul chose to cite this verse in Romans 8:36, where he certainly was thinking of undeserved suffering, possibly through Satanic persecution.

109

Strictly speaking, only verses 23 and 26 are prayers. "Awake and arise . . . rise and redeem." In between are two additional verses of complaint. Verse 24 charges God with unconcern and forgetfulness, while verse 25 describes the extreme humiliation the people of God were enduring.

The psalm ends on a slight upward swing. The mention of God's mercy, or loving-kindness (Hebrew *hesed*), reflects at least the beginning of an understanding of undeserved suffering. Psalm 136 remains in the Psalter. Twenty-six times it repeats, "For his mercy endures forever." God will never break the covenant He made by oath to His people.

PSALM 45

Psalm 45 describes a royal wedding. It is also Messianic, for Hebrews 1:8-9 quotes verses 6-7. Among other things, the title indicates that this is a love song. *Shoshanim,* meaning "lilies," is perhaps the tune to which it was sung.

Older rabbinic commentators applied the psalm to the love of God for His "wife," the nation Israel. Christian commentators apply it to the love of Christ for His bride, the Church. In this respect the psalm is very close to the Song of Solomon, which is similarly applied.

This psalm was probably composed for the wedding of a king, but several of the grandiose terms point beyond to the union of God and His people. Verse 6 is difficult in the former regard. By the same token, many of the expressions do not fit a Messianic interpretation, except by the most radical adjustment of the plain meaning. Verses 9 and 12, for example, are difficult to apply to the figures of Christ and the Church. The interpretation is preferable which sees one major lesson or application. Just as this king was super-

110

naturally endowed, so Christ is the ideal King, the very Son of God. And just as this bride abandoned her family to join her groom's, so believers are to forsake the carnal life when they are adopted into the family of God.

One additional consideration before studying the psalm verse-by-verse: Many Old Testament writers were doubtlessly not clear in their own minds about the first and second advents of Christ. They did not realize that God planned the interim of the Church age, in which Christ's kingdom would be only spiritual. When He returns, that Kingdom will then be political as well as spiritual. Many of the terms in Psalm 45 refer to the earthly, socio-political kingdom that Christ will one day set up. Mention of sword and scepter point to this millennial kingdom. Likewise the wedding is viewed in Christian theology as an eschatological event, not one which happened at the first advent.

The author of this psalm makes the first verse his introduction and the last verse his conclusion. Only those two verses contain references to this one whose "tongue is the pen of a ready writer." In a way, he is like the editor of the social page of a big city newspaper and the story of the year is this royal wedding. Hence his heart literally "bubbles up with the goodly matter." He has a story on the king!

Verses 2-9 describe the groom and verses 10-16 pertain to the bride. In ancient Semitic weddings the man was more important than the woman. He was dressed elaborately. All the guests waited to see his clothing and his attendants. The grand march played for his arrival, not the bride's—a reversal of our custom.

Accolades are exaggerated as the groom is made "king for a day." In reference to Christ, they are not exaggerated. Such praises as those in verse 2 cannot suitably fit any mere human being. Only the Son of God is fairer than the sons of men. The eternal blessing of God on the groom mentioned

111

in verse 2 is parallel to the never ending throne of verse 6 and the everlasting thanksgiving of the people in verse 17.

Verse 3 begins the description of the king's attire. The sword, though decorative in the wedding, is symbolic of his strength and his execution of justice. Verse 3 calls him the "Mighty One," a term similar to one of the epithets of the Messiah in Isaiah 9:6.

In verse 4 the king rides forth, probably on a donkey, since that animal, rather than the horse, was the customary royal mount (cf. Zec 9:9). This is one of those passages, such as Psalm 2:7-9, where the inspired penman sees both the present ministry of Christ and His eschatological triumph in the same glance. Now Christ works truth, meekness, and righteousness. Some future day His right hand will execute terrible things. Then the enemies of the Gospel will feel His arrows in their hearts (v. 5).

Verses 6 and 7 are quoted in Hebrews 1:8-9 and are applied directly to Christ to assert His superiority over angels. This New Testament commentary also bolsters the total Messianic interpretation of this psalm and is a declaration of the deity of Christ. Verses 6b and 7a list additional virtues the king possesses.

The *ivory palaces* of verse 8 may allude to the ivory inland work of walls and furniture which archaeologists have discovered in the ruins of buildings in the Holy Land (cf. 1 Ki 22:39 and Amos 3:15). A gospel song-writer has used these words to describe heaven; which Christ left when He was incarnated at Bethlehem.

Verse 9 concludes the description of the groom's side of the wedding. The references are to international participants and guests. Solomon had such international relations, but perhaps this points as well to Christ's Kingdom which will host citizens of every tribe and tongue.

The bride receives two basic instructions (vv. 10-11),

which begin the section pertaining to her. She must leave her family (v. 10) and to her husband she must cleave (v. 11). These verses underscore the believer's duty to his Lord. We were born into the family of Satan. The house of that "father" we should forget. Christ is our new Lord and loves and desires us. We must reverence Him. Just as Paul taught that a woman should submit to her husband (Eph 5:22-23), so these verses teach that a Christian should submit to the Lord Jesus Christ.

The king had female attendants (v. 9) and the bride, as well, had the daughter of Tyre in her retinue (v. 12). Although historically Solomon had good relations with the kingdom of Tyre (2 Ch 2:3 ff.), this reference may point to the universal constituency of Christ's Church.

Verses 13-14 specifically describe the bride. An ellipsis in verse 13 leaves the meaning of *within* open to guesses. Is she beautiful inside *the palace* where no one can yet see her? (cf. ASV italics). Is it that the girl is beautiful underneath all the heavy veils which customarily covered the bride? Or is she an uncomely girl who, nevertheless, has a certain inner beauty? (cf. 1 Pe 3:4).

The procession continues through verse 15 into the palace where the wedding will occur. Then verse 16 jumps ahead to speak of the offspring of this union. No longer will the bride boast in her parentage but, rather, in her children. For Christians, as ties are severed with the old life, pride is then in the groom as he begets additional "royalty" through us (cf. 1 Pe 2:9).

The poet concludes this brief but complete song with the hope that he will make it last to all generations. And as long as Psalm 45 is in our Bibles his hope is fulfilled. We who live centuries away from him still read, enjoy, and benefit from what he wrote. We are part of that people who give thanks to *the* King forever and ever.

PSALM 46

The three occurrences of *selah* divide the three stanzas of the familiar forty-sixth psalm. In fact, verses 7 and 11, which close the second and third stanzas, are identical.

Essentially all three stanzas say the same thing: Though the world is in turmoil, in our God there is quiet and safety. Martin Luther paraphrased the opening lines of this psalm in his German hymn which has come to us as "A Mighty Fortress Is Our God."

This communal psalm of confidence begins with a statement that God is both the defense and the offense of His people. He protects them as well as fights for them. That is the meaning of *refuge* and *strength*. (The *refuge* of verses 7 and 11 translate different Hebrew words.) Quite different is the confession of verse 1b from the complaint of Psalm 44:23-24.

The four stichs making up verses 2 and 3 describe violent natural catastrophes. The description sounds like a combination of earthquake, landslide, ocean storm, and flood. Without pressing the meaning of the figures, the passage simply means that no storm of life can assail us and no disaster in nature can overwhelm us since we are safe in God.

From the violence of verses 2 and 3 the psalmist turns in contrast to the tranquillity of the streams that water the city of God. Isaiah reversed these figures when he warned King Ahaz that, when he turned from the waters of Shiloah that flow softly, he would experience the flood of Assyrian soldiers who would inundate the land (Is 8:6-8).

In actuality no river flows by Jerusalem. Its water comes only from two springs, Gihon and En-Rogel. In the idyllic language of hymnody such imprecision is not only permissible but desirable to bring across the lesson intended. Both Isaiah (33:21) and Ezekiel (47:1-12) refer to a future river

114

near Jerusalem. Verse 5 completes the pacific scene begun in verse 4. God makes His home among the citizens of Zion who sing of their safety and bliss.

With verse 6a comes another scene of terror and confusion. But peace and victory come in the latter half as God merely speaks the word. By the word of His mouth He created the world and with the utterance of His voice He makes it dissolve.

The third stanza begins with an invitation to observe God's work in the world (v. 8). That is followed by a description of His work which consists of winning wars and guaranteeing peace. The bows, spears, and chariots are destroyed as He puts an end to war.

We can enjoy this hymn as poetry, but we can also anticipate the day when this will be literally true. Christ's Kingdom will enjoy a rule of absolute peace.

Verse 10 is a favorite of many people. The Hebrew word for *be still* is the same as *cease* in Psalm 37:8. The command is to let go and let God do the work. The word *know* is another very broad term in the Old Testament. Here it means "to admit," "to realize," "to acknowledge," "to experience," "to enjoy," or "to appreciate." All of God's children need to be reminded regularly of how great He is. As we fail to look at God and His Word, or fail to speak to Him in prayer, He grows smaller and weaker in our view. On the other hand, the more we study about Him, the more often we invite Him to help us, the more He will help us and the more we will *know* that He is God.

Then not only will His reputation increase in our eyes, but the unconverted of the world will also be led to recognize and exalt Him. When God is given a chance to prove His love and might, we will be prompted and required to confess that the Lord of hosts is with us, the God of Jacob is our refuge.

115

PSALM 47

Psalm 47 is a short hymn which was probably sung at one of the annual festivals. A *selah* divides the work roughly in half, but the content is quite homogeneous throughout. The psalmist may have had the literary device of chiasmus in mind, for a number of repeated words suggest such an inverted parallelism. *Peoples* occurs in the first and last verses. Verses 2-4 and 7-8 are linked by the terms *king of all the earth and nations.* That leaves verses 5-6 as the middle of the psalm.

The opening verse hints at the exuberance with which God's ancient people praised Him. In view of the disdain many Christians have for handclapping and other expressions of rhythm accompanying hymn singing, and in view of the total inappropriateness of applause for God in our worship patterns, this verse is an interesting commentary on the way God's chosen people worshiped Him in olden times. Perhaps the Church is not excited enough about the things God does. Maybe our worship is too solemn. On the other hand, worship must ever seek that delicate balance which Psalm 2:11 spells out:

> Serve the LORD with fear,
> And rejoice with trembling.

The second verse of Psalm 47 immediately turns from the ebullition of the worshipers to the terror and greatness of the Worshiped. Never let it be forgotten that He about whom gospel ditties are sung is also the great and terrible King over all the earth.

In verses 3 and 4 ancient Israelites reflected on what God did for them. Primarily He chose the patriarchs from a sea of heathendom and then brought their descendants into the promised land.

116

With verse 5 the praise is in more general terms. The use of the words "go up" has led some commentators to see this as an enthronement psalm. Such songs were used by the nations neighboring Israel when the statue of their god was paraded through the city and deposited in his sanctuary. If such a background influenced this psalm, it certainly was written from a more enlightened theology. The God in this psalm is the God of all the earth who reigns over the nations and who owns the shields of the earth (vv. 8, 9). He is not a local deity who is revered by only one city-state.

"Sing praises" occurs four times in verse 6 and once more in verse 7. It sounds like it may have been a chant that the laity on the sidelines sang as the priests and the Levites executed their functions in the temple precincts.

Verses 8-9 have an eschatological ring to them. References to nations, peoples, the whole earth, and God's universal rule usually point to the future era when men from many lands and languages will join the covenant people of God, and God's Kingdom truly will be worldwide (cf. Zec 14:9).

PSALM 48

As Psalm 47 praised the God of Zion, so Psalm 48 exalts the Zion of God. It may be the psalm was written to commemorate the salvation of the city from the planned attack of Sennacherib in 701 B.C. (cf. Is 36, 37). Verses 4 and 5 in particular support such a guess. Other Bible students wonder if this psalm does not commemorate the rebuilding of Jerusalem by Nehemiah (Neh 12:27). Verses 12-13 bolster that suggestion.

Since Jerusalem is the city God chose for His name to

dwell in, it partakes of the praise that is given to God Himself. Just as the name, the remembrance, and the deeds of God get praise, so too His city is honored. Although some of the epithets are exaggerated, Zion, to use the poetic name, was a beautiful place.

The psalmist is careful not to let the city, apart from its God, become the focus of worship. Such a form of idolatry is always imminent when the place of worship is beautiful and tends to replace the Person of worship. Some people choose a church on the primary basis of architecture. All bragging about the church building and its attendant facilities runs the risk of the sin of idolatry. Zion is only beautiful and glad because the temple is there and in that temple the God of heaven made His earthly sanctuary.

The opening verse focuses praise on God and then the subject turns to the city situated on God's holy mountain. It took a poet to pen the words of Verse 2. Although Jerusalem is set on a hill it is only 2,500 feet above sea level. Located on the spine of the north-south ridge, it is also in the morning shadow of the Mount of Olives which rises 100 feet higher.

Beginning with verse 3 is an account of some deliverance which God wrought for the city. According to verse 3 He was known, i.e., appreciated or recognized as the real refuge for the people. So when hostile kings plotted an attack, they suddenly retreated. The psalmist does not tell what amazed and dismayed them, but for some reason they began to shake and writhe as a travailing woman. The figures of verse 7 even more graphically magnify their fear as the hostile kings are compared to wind-wrecked, oceangoing ships.

Selah concludes verse 8, which is a summary to the foregoing incident. That act of supernatural deliverance elicited a pledge of unwavering faith from the citizens of Jerusalem.

Particularly in the temple of Jerusalem did God reside.

118

According to verse 9, every sight of it prompted thoughts of God's loving-kindness and mercy. Is that what we think of when we drive by our church? Or does the sight of the building remind us instead of problems, impossible people, and preachers? Would that every church house moved us to speak the words of verse 10:

> According to your name, O God,
> So is your praise to the ends of the earth.
> Your right hand is full of righteousness.

In highly figurative terms the citizens of the city are urged to rejoice. Of course a mountain cannot be glad, and the command is not just to the women of one tribe.

Despite the detailed accounts of the temple and the many references to the city of Jerusalem, it still is difficult to reconstruct them as they stood in Old Testament times. But from verses 12 and 13 they must have been both beautiful and strong.

Some modern translations have altered the traditional last words of Psalm 48 from *unto death* to *forever*. This may be correct for several reasons. *Unto death* does not fit with the sense and makes a bad parallel line. The Greek translators of the Old Testament read it as meaning *eternity*. This is entirely possible with a text that has no vowels. The two Hebrew words can also make another word which is the *alamoth* in the title of Psalm 46 (cf. 1 Ch 15:20). So the expression may belong with the title of Psalm 49 and not at the end of Psalm 48. Or it may be read as *forever*.

Whether the traditional text or the emended one is correct, the truth is not altered. God is our God and our guide, now, at death, beyond, and to eternity.

PSALM 49

Psalm 49 is a wisdom psalm. In it the wise are warned against trusting in wealth. It will perish as the rich man whose fate is no better than an animal's.

The first four verses are the introduction. After that, only in verses 5 and 15 does the psalmist speak of himself. The body of the work is in verses 6-14, while the five concluding verses are didactic and repetitive.

Verses 1-4 each contain pairs of very strict parallels. The summons to attention goes out to everyone of every class of society. The sage announces his intention of speaking in a proverbial form, while accompanying himself on the harp.

Verse 5 is an interlude and a transition. It sounds like the poet is eliminating himself from the upcoming indictment of the rich and foolish. The things that ordinarily shake up other people will not move him.

The actual message begins in verse 6. The subjects are sketchily described by the two synonymous phrases of verse 6, and the acts they cannot do are spelled out in verse 7. The psalmist is obviously saying that money cannot buy off God. The word "redeem" (v. 7) is not used in the economic sense but in the spiritual. This truth hardly needs repeating—the rich, either with money or good deeds, cannot produce enough to pay the cost of a soul. If it took the shed blood of Christ to satisfy the just demands of God, then surely material means are inadequate. Not only are they insufficient but they are not even comparable, since the spiritual dimension demands another medium of payment. Furthermore, there may be a link, as often there is elsewhere in the Old Testament, between evil (v. 5) and wealth (v. 6). Often the rich are so only because of exploitation, bribery, and crooked business practices. Certainly it is not always so, for else-

120

where in Scripture certain rich men are described as commendable and godly (e.g., Abraham, Solomon, and the centurion of Mt 8).

The sentence begun in verse 6 actually continues through verse 9 (it may even have started in verse 5). The additional message of verse 8 is that no amount of money will ever suffice for the price of a soul. And the additional message of verse 9 is that a rich man cannot preserve himself from death and corruption.

The book of Ecclesiastes, in a manner of speaking, is a commentary on verse 10. Rich or poor, wise or foolish, all men die, and that which they have must be left behind. How or by whom their inheritance will be used is something hard to control.

Some people build monuments to themselves—gravestones, churches, schools—and even name streets, cities, and countries after themselves. Such means do not preserve their souls (v. 11) regardless of how hard they work or how rich they become. Verse 12 repeats the inevitable truth—men die like beasts. This verse forms a conclusion to the first stanza and is repeated at the end of the psalm.

It is folly for a person to think he will not die. It is stupid to welcome the congratulations of men without reckoning with the judgment of God. The end is like that of a sheep in the slaughterhouse. Houses and wealth will be consumed in the fires of destruction.

In the middle of verse 14 are a glimmer of truth and a sparkle of hope for those who are trusting in something other than wealth: "The upright shall have dominion over them in the morning." This is one of the relatively few references to the afterlife in the Old Testament. *In the morning* can refer to nothing other than life after death. In that great day all injustices and all inequities will be rectified. At the

121

great reckoning the upright will plead the death and life of the crucified Son of God as their redemption.

That ray of light in verse 14 undoubtedly prompted the personal testimony of verse 15. While the rich man could not redeem his own soul (vv. 7-8) the psalmist declares that God will redeem his (v. 15).

Because of this truth and in the light of eternity, we are enjoined not to be afraid of the rich man in the big house. Just a little reflection will remind us of the brevity and futility of life not lived by faith. The rich may have many friends and be happy while he lives (v. 18). But in a few brief years he will join his ancestors in the grave, where there is no light.

Verse 20, which is similar to verse 12, concludes the second stanza as well as the whole psalm on the dismal note which must be continually sounded in warning to unbelievers.

> Man that is in honor and understands not
> Is like the beasts that perish.

PSALM 50

Asaph is connected with twelve psalms, 50 and 73-83. He is undoubtedly the singer mentioned in 1 Chronicles 15:19 and elsewhere. He served the tabernacle during the time of David. Most of the psalms bearing his name are longer praise psalms, but some include imprecations. Others, such as this one, are really sermons directed to God's people.

It is not hard to understand why Asaph, a professional singer, also should be a composer. But we cannot be sure of what the word *of* means in the expressions "a psalm *of* Asaph" or *"of* David."

Here is one outline for the psalm:

Introduction (1-6)
God's dissatisfaction with insincere sacrifice (7-21)
Warning and promise (22-23)

A *selah* concludes the introduction, which has two thrusts to it. First is the announcement of God's coming. Second is the summons to saints to stand trial. Although the opening couple of verses sound like a praise psalm, the fire and tempest of verse 3 suggest that God has unpleasant business in mind. In verse 4 that purpose is specifically stated: He is to judge His people.

In verse 5 the worshipers are summoned to give account of their integrity in the matter of sacrificing. They must have been unfaithful to the covenant they had made with God or such a charge would not be warranted. The use of the word *saints* may be a sarcastic, tongue-in-cheek insult. That Hebrew word, when not a participle, is usually rendered *lovingkindness, faithfulness,* or *mercy*. God, the Judge, is about to accuse His people of not possessing these qualities.

The body of the psalm has two parts. Verse 7 introduces the long quotation of God in verses 8-15. Verse 16 introduces God's words against the wicked (vv. 16b-23). The first part is an attack on insincere sacrifice. The second half is broader and is an attack on unethical practices among the people of God.

God makes it very clear that He neither needs nor really wants sacrifice. In this respect the psalm shares the insightful theology of Isaiah and Amos. God's first requirement is integrity. Sacrifices only show a worshiper's overt obedience.

Even for Christians it is often easier to do the overt thing rather than have a heart right toward God. To some people, regular attendance at the church services is more important than the "weightier matters of the law." To others, giving to missions is far easier than being a missionary to unsaved relatives and neighbors. So for the ancient people of Israel, sacrifice replaced true service, and burnt offerings substituted for inward piety.

The point is obvious: God does not drink the blood nor eat the meat of sacrifices but He examines the motives of the believer. More important to Him is the sacrifice of thanksgiving and the paying of vows, i.e., the keeping of promises. 1 Samuel 15:22 and Psalm 51:16, 17 also emphasize this basic truth.

God concludes the first half of the psalm with an invitation to call on Him in time of trouble (v. 15). "Let me deliver you and you glorify me," God says.

The second major section of the psalm (vv. 16-21) is much more caustic and accusing. Perhaps the two sections are tied together with this line of reasoning: there are certain sins for which there is no prescribed sacrifice. So the inadequacy of the old sacrificial system is especially shown by the nature of these offenses. Among them are hateful attitudes (v. 17), sharing with thieves and adulterers (v. 18), lying (v. 19), and slander (v. 20).

The twenty-first verse culminates the list by charging that the people hold to the misconception that God is like men who tolerate sin and accept bribes. His silence, however, does not indicate His forgiveness but only His patience. God is waiting until the cup of iniquity is full. Then He proceeds to warn before it is too late.

The conclusion (vv. 22-23) is two-fold. Verse 22 is a warning to the wicked against coming judgment, and verse 23 is a promise to the righteous. It is the offering of true thanksgiving that glorifies God. And the one who watches his step and examines his way of life (*conversation,* KJV) sees the salvation of God.

Moody Press, a ministry of the Moody Bible Institute, is designed for education, evangelization and edification. If we may assist you in knowing more about Christ and the Christian life, please write us without obligation to: Moody Press, c/o MLM, Chicago, Illinois 60610.